Charlie Farquharson's

Histry of
Canda *

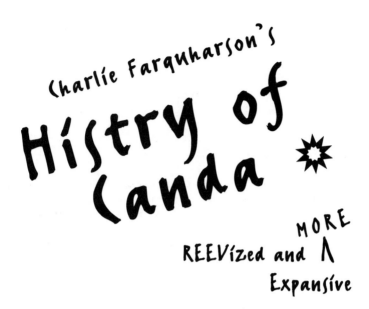

Charlie Farquharson's
Histry of Canda ✴

REEVized and ^MORE
Expansive

As told to

Valeda Drain Farquharson

when it was too wet to plow

MACMILLAN CANADA

TORONTO

Canadian Cataloguing in Publication Data

Harron, Don, date.
  Charlie Farquharson's Histry of Canda
ISBN 0-7715-9983-8

1. Canada — History — Humor. I. Title.

PS8565.A66C48 1992   971'.00207   C92-094314-4   PR9199.3.H377C48 1992

1 2 3 4 5 JD 96 95 94 93 92

Design by Counterpunch/Linda Gustafson
Cover photo by Edan Robins

Macmillan Canada wishes to thank the Canada Council
for supporting its publishing program.

Macmillan Canada
A Division of Canada Publishing Corporation
Toronto, Ontario, Canada

Printed in Canada

To Ben and Zoe
my grandchildren
in the hope that
they have a Canada
to grow up in

✴ Contents

Part í yí yí ❁ 97

Epic Log ❁ 171

✴ Pro Log

I writ a Histry of Canda twenny yeer ago and I figger it's now time to bring it up to dait while we still has a country to tock about. Canda has now add a quarter to its Sintenniel in '67 and this yeer is also being celibated as the haffa millenema (five hunderth analversry) of yer uncuvvering of Amerka. Any buddy who nose Canajun histry reelizes that Kriss Stuffer Clumbuss was nuthin' but a John-cum-Laidly in the uncuvvery bizness. Him and his co-hores – Nino, Pinto, Sandy, and Maria – was reely lookin' fer the gold of Injure when they happen to bump into the topical ile of Sam Saliva Door hard by Nassaw in yer Grand Bananas.

So Clumbuss never reely got to Amerka atall, but only as far as yer edge of yer Carbean in his West Undys. 'Sides, I dunno how you kin claim to disscuver a hole hemmysfeer that was alreddy filled with mebby a hunderd millyun people. In later trips his croose ships stopped in some of the saim tooryist traps them wintry luvboats do nowadaze, naimly Poorty-Reeky-o and yer Dumminny-kick-a-can Republican. But this was after our Granbanks had bin pride open by Bask'n Porchygeese fishymen and they bin takin' regler depossets frum us ever since. Reesmirchers has recently uncover a 1398 cannon in the mud of Looeyburg. Histerians say it was left there by a Scot name of Prince Hennery Sinkler. That's the dait, 1398, not the price, so that old fowl peece was left on yer Cape Breton almost a centurion before Clumbuss. Some septics say a Scot wood never leeve anything beehind, but yuh kin see it fer yerself in the old Fartress musuleum of them Looeyburgers.

Smatter of fack, Newfyland was visit morn fore hunnert yeer afore *that* by Vikers, them see-going Scandalnavyans with the horny hats. And long before them hairy pillagers got round to laying the inhibitants waist, there was sposed to of bin a liddle Bennydickteen munk called Saint Bren-gun. He paddled his own liddle round bottom in a wicker boat all the ways frum Ire-Land to Noo Brunsick about ate hunnerd A.T. (Atlantical Time ... haff a senchry later in Newfunland.)

So when yiz gits rite down to it, all these so-call discuvverers was finding a land that had bin alreddy inhibited fer at leest ten, mebby twenny-five, thousand yeers before that. The first famlys of Canda was reely dinashores, Brontysores and the odd Tronto-soreass Recks. They lived in a topical climax up in yer Artix, but sumbuddy terned off the thermalstat and brung on yer Ice Age, and insted of bean in heat, Canda becum frigid and uninhibited at the same time. The first yuman beans to cum to Canda as immygrunts was morer less the same bunch as is tryna git in now frum Honk Cong. They cum acrost the Go-bye dessert and hedded tord our parts as soon as they got their berings strait. I guess they had their eyes opened when they hit our shores, fur it was after that they turned into Injuns and Innerwits.

I don't care what that Jock Parrysound sez, the original abridge-nall groops is distinkly the two foundering nations of our country.

Part 1 ☀

✳ Yer First Sittyzens

Now there ain't no sitch thing as yer averidge Injun. As far as a commin langridge is consern, them differnt tribes woodna known what each uther was talkin' about. Yer West Coaster, Hyeedas, and Squeamish is a diffrunt kettle of fish frum them Marrytimer McMacs hoose lifestile was mostly dulse. Yer Quackydoodles up yer Queen Sharlits was so rich they had slaves, and they lived pritty good offa

Gittin' buffaload on snowshoos

yer smoke sammon and yer cavvy-R. Yer Planes Injun had never seen a sammon, but as long as he was knee-deep in buffalo he was in the chips. After white men cum, them plain Injians was left with next to nuthin' but discouragin' words, and not a buffalo heard in site.

Yer Ontaryan naytiff peeple was the farmers of the bunch. They had feelds of corn, squarsh and beans, tho it was their wimmen that dun most of the feeldwork. Their braves was off in the bush chasin' yer fur-boring animals on snowshoos.✱ Yer Cue-

✿ FEETAL
FEETNOTE

Don't ast me ware them animals got ther snowshoos. I jist copeed that detale strait frum my old scool histry book.

3
✿

beck Injians was big birch-bark strippers, and after a hard day's strippin' they'd put on a lotta make-up, go to their lodge meetin' and dance with eech uther. Takes all kinds.

Birch-bark strippers

When it cum to plittickle orgynization yer Red man was senchrys ahed of yer White if you look at them Eery-quoits. They was reely Moehawks, Oh-Niters, Kayugers, Sennycuz, and Onan-doggers but when they all fot in the same leeg they was call yer Five Nations. When them Tusky Roarers from North Carliner was kick out by the Chair-o-keys, and adapted by yer Five, then they all becum noan as yer Sex Nations.

But what they dun after dark was their own bizness. The manething is they was way ahed of us in guvmint. At a time when Yerp was fulla kings and queans dickytating to their common peeples, them Eeryquoit had a real Parlamint ware everybuddy, incloodin the wimmin, cood speek their piece. That's becuz in their sassiety wimmen had the vote and was reely in charge of the yewconomy. They also had the job of deepozing any of the Saychums (Cheefs) who wasn't doin it rite by them. This kinda derangement is what the texbook calls mate-tree-ark-all and it's commoner than you'd think, speshully round our house.

Their Parlmint bilding was called the Longhouse. I dunno if it was named after the speaches in it, but it worked pritty much like Questing Peeriod in our Common House. A lotta our democrappic idears cum frum them old-time Abie-originals, but I don't think we have got them rite yet. They even had nomnating convenshuns fer leeders and caucusses fer to help them make their deecisions. All this pubic speeking was dun orly, as oppose to our sistern witch rites everything down yeer after yeer in yer Hanserd, so that our pollytishuns kin remember what they sed. Our sassiety is not so much orly retentiv as it is anually.

They had Thanksgivering too, longafore them Puritanicals got off their Rock at Plimmuth and was saved frum starvation that first winter by the lokel Massachewsitts Amerken-Injun Food Bank. Them Pillgrims had ther first taist of turky, crambury soss, sweet pataters and punkin pie. And what did that relijuss bunch give them in return? All the cumforts of civilly-ization: nives, guns, smallpocks, meazles, and tuber-colossus, to say nothing about the demon-rarer rum.

❋ Yer Norse Sagass

So far as yer Yerp, yer Azure, and yer Africker in them old-time times was consern, Canda was purty much on yer Continental Shelf. Nobody in yer forn parts knew or cared much who or where our place was. That hasn't changed all that much, I guess.

The first fellas to sneak away for a weekend in our outports was them big blond sailers yer Norses. They was hangin' 'round Iceland (not to be confused with a skatin' rink of the same name in Port Carlin') when they decided to see how far they could get on one galleon. They got as far as yer Greenland, which is darn good mileage. If they'da brung a furmometer with 'em, they'da never called it Greenland; more like Blueland – it was cold enuff to freeze the knots offa blue spruce.

One of them Icemen, Barny Herjolffson, mist his stop and got blown off course by a storm, and all that passing wind took him to a place jist off Labbydoor, which look pritty gud to this Ice and Snowman. Insted of friggid waists it had trees and bushys and grapes swingin' on the vines. Barny called the place Antsy Meddows cuz they was ankshuss to git back home and tell their boss about this new found land.

Their boss was Airick yer Red, but he was too bizzy developpin' his Greenland Akers fer to check out this new projeck, so he sent his Number One Son, Leaf yer Lucky fer to check it out. Leaf musta had some Norse's horses cuz he bilt a blacksmithshop at Antsy Meddows witch was unvaled by Norwejun archy-ollogists about twenny, thurty yeer ago. Leaf spent mosta his time hanging round Sinjons on weak-ends hopin' to live up to his name. He tride James Bay too, but he never cum up with a Grate Wail of a projeck, so he hit out fer the States and finely ended up in Minnyapples ware he becum yer first Norse Amerken. He later dide and becum known as Leaf yer Lucky Stiff. His dad, Eric yer Red went down the eestcoast past Newfyland and settle in Road Iland ware he soon becum Eric yer Ded, but he still has famly in them parts. You probly heard of them Road Iland Reds.

The resta them Greenlanders went back to Iceland to attend the openin' of the latest vullcanoe. Histerians say that by the end of yer tense senchry them Vyekings was havin a deecline and fallout of their civilly-ization, and they got the valhalla outta their summer cottidges in Greenland and retreeted as far as Stockhome. But our own frictional histerian Furry Mowit thinks that them Norse evaders was druv away by a naytif peeple called B-Uttocks.* The lokels

Them poor B-Uttox becum extincted in yer nineteenth senchry after being bounty-hunted to deth by the new Newfylanders frum the Berdish Iles.

(who had bin in Newfland fifteen hunnert yeers before them Vyekings got there) fot back and the upshat was that aginst this race, the Norses cum in secund.

✳ Yer Godfather of Our Country

Never mind Clumbuss, us Canajuns was found by our own Eyetalian! Do you mind John Cabot? Sounds like he come from Boston, but he was another one of them Marrytime MafiasCo. Since he was workin' fer the Anglish King, Henry Seven*, they made him change his name to somethin' they could pernounce 'stead of Geo-Vanna Club-Auto.

✿ ROYL FEETNOTE

Henry Seven, he wasn't the fella had the six wives, Anne Balloon, Jane Arden and all them others and later died of gunnerrear. That was next year's model, Henry Eight.

Now, King Henry sent our John to look fer a root to the Far East, and Cabot's trail led from the port of Bristle strait to Newfieland. So he done what the King told him, 'cause, by gol, if St. John's ain't yer Far East, I don't know what is.

He brung along his son, Sebastian Cabot, too, makin' it a family affair. Sebastian he was in the reg'lar bizness of takin' credit fer his father's acheevments, and he done so good at it he retired even before his father got pensioned off. Which was only ten pounds a year after King Henry found out his tame Eyetalian had discovered Newfieland 'stead of Sam Arcand and Ind. Them Anglish figgered that this mistake was a whopper. Which is too bad 'cause yer St. John's is a purty darn good port in any storm. And ice free too.* It's too bad Henry din't b'leeve in cod.

✿ COLD FEETNOTE

Ice free. Drinks fifty cents. Open Sundys too.

Them Porchygeese fishymen sure did. They bin smelting fer our fish around the Martimes since time in memoriam, long afore John Cabot tride to grab it. But you take yer averadge fish man, he don't mind talkin' bout yer fish what got away, but he's not gonna tell anyone where he gits the ones that don't. When it cums to droppin his hooks and pullen 'em in, he's no loose lipper; he'll clam up like yer small mouth bass. So whose to say how long them Porchygeese bin gittin' hevvy net profits? Mebby we should extend our 200 mile limit about three thousand extry miles so we kin play in their backyard pool for a change.

✳ Yer Great Breton, Jack Carter*

I b'leeve she'd be about 15:34 Eastern Standard when Jack Carter set sail from the port of St. O'Malley lookin' fer the Spacific Rimmers of Far Camay. Now you'd think by this time anybody with any sents'd head strait fer yer Medium-Terranian and the Sue-us Canal or even round yer Cake of Good Hoke hard by Joanna's Burg. But thanks to them Porchygeese and their fishy tails, Jack Carter lit out strait fer our Happy Fishin' Grounds, probly dropt by them eyelets of Sam Pee-air and Micky-long.

But he went a lot furthern that. I dunno how many Chinamen he expeckted to find goin' thru yer Straits of Belial, but he wound up down yer Sin Lorrent Seeway looking fer them Himmel-upanlaya Mountings and the gold of yer Taj Mahar. He did find a hole passle of wigwarms at Static-Coma (Cue-beck City) run by a Injian Chieftess Donna

Jimmy Sweeze appell Jock Carshay!
(Hi! My name is Jack Carter. Can I squeeze your apples?)

Coma. She got him outta town by tellin' him to go West, oldman, and mebby he'd find gold.

That Chieftess even got out her own canew and bowd wile he paddled her stern on the way down the river. They spent the weak-end in Muntry-all (then called Hotcha Lager) witch even back then was a pritty big town. But Carter was still lookin' fer Injure and Chiner. He run into some rappids witch he called La Sheen (witch is French fur China). That's as far as he got with Donna Coma. Jack wanted to go all the way with her, say as far as down river to Tibet (reely Gana-nockyou-up) but he warnt that good in a canew and couldn't pass his rappids test.

Back in Static Coma, Carter tride givin' away cheep beeds and the Indians gave him scurfy in ex-change. So Carter shang-hide ten Static Comos, left in a rush but didden cum back fer sex yeers. Nine outta ten of his Injun "gests" in the meentime dide of some French diseese. When Jack cum back he never brung the loan serf-viver with

YER POLER BARE PASSAGE

him, cuz he figgerd she'd spill the beens when he told
Donna Coma that all ten was too happy on them Parse
boolyvards drinkin' sidewalk caffays fer to cum back home
and slum. Them Injuns didden bleeve him fer a minit.

It was a long time before enny white man tride to set
up shop in Canda agin. That man was Sam Plain and when
he got there sexty yeers later, there wernt no Static Coma
or Hotcha Lager. They'd bin wipe out by a full-fledge epi-
dermic of small pocks that Jack Carter had brung over
along with his beeds. He probly figgered it was a fare traid
fer all that scurfy he took back to Fran's.

✵ Yer Poler Bare Passage

I guess the main reason yer av'rage Canadian has been
infeerior in his complecks is the fack that nobody ever really wanted to visit us in the first place. Them exploiters was
all lookin' fer the gold and spicys of yer Tartery and yer
Southeast Azure and were desprit to find away around us.
Now why anybody would go further north and west fer to
git south and east don't make no cents. 'Cept
to yer Anglish mebbe.* The first few times
they tried to give us a by-pass they kept
bumpin' into yer Labbydoor. So bein' ex-scen-
trick they went further north, figgerin' on
runnin' up around yer pole fer to git to yer
topical places with the hot climacks. You take
yer av'rage Anglishman he'll allus do it the
hard way, like standin' up in a hammock. Mind you they're
a pretty friggid bunch anyways, havin' not bin in central

✿ STUBBERN
FEETNOTE

Tippical bull-head peo-
ple, yer Anglish, says
Valeda who's mostly
Scotch but still won't
touch it.

heat since the Roamins was in their gloamin' 'bout 55 B.B.C.

But there was a lotta crazy Angled-Sacksons up in our Artick all at the same time – Humpy Filbert, Marty Furbisher, and Look Focks – but the jimmy dido what become a big name was Henry Hudson, who has since become a bay, a blankit, and a car that's now obsolene.

Bay days

Now Henry he went far. He got past yer Bafflin Island and yer Straights of Umgawa till he got into that big dead end which was his namesake by posterior. Mind you, Hudson's bay had no company yet and yer Moose Factory wasn't turnin' out moose, and the crew wanted to git to where there was somethin' to do on shore leave like Goose Bays. But Henry he drug them all down to the James Bay hard by yer Timmins and Cockran, and tole 'em he planned to winter it out till fly-time fishin' thru the ice. Well the crew wanted to spend their winter in a Corner Brook bar fishin' thru the ice fer marsheeno cherries. They up and held a mutininny and was gonna make Henry and his son Rock* walk yer divin' board, but it was so cold they woulda broke their necks on the ice, so the crew jist left them with abandon.

✿ SON-OF-A FEETNOTE

Valeda douts his name was that. Let's jist say he was a chop off the old block.

Now if you look up yer histry directomies, they'll try and tell you nobody don't know what happen to Henry and the little Hudson. But my gol, lookit yer map hard by New Jersey. It's sure oblivious to me that Henry left the ice bizness and went into yer down-river trade where he finely come out down there jist this side of yer Statute of Libertations. He may of bin the first, but he sure warn't the last of us to retire and head south.

✳ In Yer Hat

There was allus somethin' fishy 'bout the start of yer Canda, with all them Porchygeese net-minders draggin' theirselves around, and even the Spanish fly-casting all over the place. It was gittin' so crowded with forners 'bout this time, yer Grand Banks tride to close at three o'clock but they're now cot in the overdrafts and undertoes of a shortedge of credit cods.

In fack, Newfieland purty near become one of yer Spanish Might'n Main possessions till one of them Anglish free-booties, Sir Humpy Filbert, come bargin' into St. John's, jumped their ships, stuck his nose in their focussles, and snatched the catch in yer Spanyard's hatch. This he done all in the good name of Queen Bessie, which used to be virgin till it was lost in the mists of her time.

Now if any of them forners had done the same thing to us, we woulda beat about their bush callin' them all sortsa things. We'd a figgered them fer plain pirates and probly give them a whiff of grape-nuts on their broadside. But since we done it ourselves, us Angled-Sacksons genally call it yer explore-atory research 'stead of what it really is – jist another buck-an-ear wavin' his skull and crotchbones.

But them Bask fishymen was tired anyways of exposin' theirselves to our wind and weather, and they was longin' to head fer home as soon as they dried their cod-pieces.

Seems nobody ever wanted to hang around our place till somebody found out there was money to be made in the hat bizness.

Yes sir, Leave it to Beaver fer to settle up Canda. This dam animal is really the Mother of Our Country on accounta the hair on its back bein' so desecrative. Purty soon all yer high muckymucks and sassiety people in Yerp wanted to git felt.

Now you've heard of yer Paris hats, strickly allah Mode.* The wife she bought one once when she was had by cuzzins down to Paris hard by Brantford. Well, it was them French city Parisites before ev'rybody else is allus intrusted in what's *à la mode*. And yer beaver soon become Number One on yer Hat parade.

> ☼ CRANIAL FEETNOTE
>
> Valeda sez her hat was fer sure. She got ice cream on it.

✳ Yer Pork Royl

I guess one of yer most poplar games in the old-time France was Trivial Pursoots. But next to them would be Mynopply. The rools was set by yer French King-pin Henry Four (not to be confused with yer Birtish King Henry Four, what was sub-divisioned by Shakespeer into two parts).

Yer French rooler he figgered the only way to play the game was to corner yer beaver market out of sheer immigrance by makin' them traders and trappers stay there thru the winter. If you keep yer trap shut all winter you miss a lotta fur pieces. Henry figgered in the summertime them trappers could take to farmin' since farmin' is considered by most of yer Middle-Aged Kings to be the backbone of yer hole civilly-eyezation. And I s'pose they was right, give or take a coupla inches.

Anyways, yer first settlement was bilt in a ring 'round yer AnalAppolis Basin and called yer Pork Royl. That was on accounta the King sent along a coupla tons of fat-back fer to last them thru till mebbe yer twenty-fourth of May. Well sir, by the time that day come 'round, ev'rybody was sick of pork and nobody was speakin' to one another, they was so salty.

Too bad, 'cause when they started out some of the times they had had was good. 'Specially when they all took orders fer yer Good Cheer, a kinda after-hours club set up by their Good Cheerleader, yer Seer de Months, to keep all their spirits flowin' reg'lar. His work was later carried on somethin' fierce in Montreal by yer Seer de Molson who brung on yer Golden Aged.

Marg Lescargot, one of yer Good Cheerios, she got up a concert called yer Theatre of Neptoon, which keeps on till this day hard by Hallyfacks.

Yer Order of Good Cheer

Anyways, come fly-time all them Pork Roylers was ready to pack up their charter and take flight back home. I guess mebbe they'd had enough of yer capitalist's punishment, 'cause they jist said "The hell with Novy Scotia, let yer dark and dreary mountings be..." (which was later made famous by the wife's favourite mezzanine soprano, Kathleen McCinnamon, the one who's claimed to have the voice of an Anglo).

You can still see the ring them Pork Roylers left 'round the Basin, but that AnalAppolis never got settled down fer another twenty year, when yer Scotch was moved in and gave proof to the locals they had the stuff to last. About ninety proof.

✳ Yer Founderer

Not all of them Royl Porkers went back to Fran's. Wun of them, Sam Sham Plain had his heart set on permanint resonance. He was thinkin' of mebby sum-
merin' in Cape Cod but his Martime friends sent him up the Sin Lorrent River jist like Jack Carter. Sam and his little bunch was a distink minorty when he got to Cuebec, but he had wun advantage that the naytif majorty was without: a gun.

Sam bleeve in the old sayin' that yew kin git more with a smile and a kind word and a gun than yew can with a smile and a kind word. So he stuck to his guns, then traded them to the Injians fur furs. Sam dun well with the gun-runnin', and them Al-Gonk-You-Win Injuns kept pelting him with ther beavers. They invited him to a party with some

Sam Plain shooting up with his sex-tante

Eeryquoits frum New York. It turned out to be a war party and Sam showed off with his old repeater.

Mind you, Sam Plain interjuiced some good things too. He riz up the first high-rise in down-town Cuebec city. It was a superiory complecks called yer Habit-tot on accoun-ta they even took in couples with child.

But one child they disallowed in there was Mrs. Sam Plain who was only a twelve-years-old miner when they was married. Now twelve in them days was sooner than yer "age of intent" and so fer quite a time she had to stay in France, bein' kept outta Cuebec by their well-known Padlock Law.

Now Sam felt this law was a frustrate thing to keep him from comin' to be yer Father of New French. He was so cheesied off that when some more Anglish free-booties dropped their ankers on Cuebec, Sam left the hole thing to them and went back to Paris on yer passionate leave.

But he come back in a coupla years after them Anglish got freebooted out, and this time he brung his teeny-age wife with him, but he was smart enuff to include along one of them Jesyouwait priests as baby-sitter.

I dunno whether married life agreed with Sam or no, but it was about this time he started leavin' his Habit-tot a lot and spendin' summers with the boys up on Georgian Bay. First he went up river on the Ottawa and tried to paddle past the site of yer Common House but was turned back by a great wind.*

The wife she claims Sam Plain musta stopped by Parry Sound one day fer lunch 'cause she found a small momentum of his a few years back on the fourth concession down by the town line. It had an old rusty knob fallin' to pieces, and when she took it to our Town Librarium fer to find out what it was, he told her Sam Plain musta used it fer a sextant. Valeda's never bin back to that liberry since.*

✿ OTTAWAR FEETNOTE

Valeda sez that wind still hits us, not off yer Common House but yer Gorgin' Bay. Our hens turn their backs to that wind and lay the saim aigs six or seven times.

✿ ARTIFACTUAL FEETNOTE

The sextant is now restin' on its lorls in the museum in Parry Sound.

✳ Yer Man on His Terre

Cuebec City got kinda quiet when Sam and his Plainsmen was busy tourin' 'round the stix, so them as stayed behind thought they should think up another place it would be fun to go on a weekend.

The fella what really thunk it up, his name was yer Seer de Masonsnerves. The King sent him out with some of his palisades fer to bild this place, Ville Marie, outta wood logs and fur posts. Jist the thing fer to catch yer passin' tooriest.*

Masonsnerves he was allus a big booster fer to git visitors fer to come and see his mountin. That Jesyouwait priest brung over by Sam Plain got all his R.C. friends to come. So many of them in fack that it was hard to keep up with the holy orders.

I figger about this time there was as many habits and hassocks as there was reg'lar inn-habitants. Seems ev'rybody all of a sudden got the old time religion.

Now you'd think them Anglican Londoners down in them Boston States and yer R.C. Parishioners would git along jist fine, and probly organize a taffy pull after the Bingo. And they woulda too if they'd stuck to farmin', cause come thrashin' time everybody helps everybody else no matter how hard you can't stand 'em. Sides, everybody loves everybody after six differnt pieces of pie.

✧ ANALVERSARY FEETNOTE

Muntry-all has celibated yer 350th analversary of its floundering and the Chambers frum Commerce ast the lokels to smile at visiters ta mark the occasion. It'd be a lot better if they reverse that bill 178 that sez yuh cant put sines in English outside yer store. Mosta the visiters is Yanks who speek only broken Amurrican.

☼ BIBLICKLE
FEETNOTE

Valeda sez I cooda
lerned that before I
started if I'd read the
Good Book: "It is a hon-
our without profit in
our own country."

But in them days they was still havin' a fur-fer-all. With all them expensive coats runnin' 'round on four legs nobody had a mind to be hoein' and hayin' and geein' and hawin'. They knew two hundert years ago what I'm jist learnin': that farmin' is a downright loosin' preposition.[12]

☀ Yer Great Intender

By now we're up to King Louie, Fourteen, yer son-king. He took over the bizness from his father, Louie the unlucky (Thirteen). Young Louie he decided to git things settled over to yer New France. He sent out a boss sibilant servant called yer Super Intender.

That'd be Tellon

Now yer Super Intender, Jean-yer-Baptist Tellon, he figgered the best way to keep people down on the Cuebec farms after they'd seen Paree was to give them all guvermint land grabs. First off, he made some older inn-habitants into Seniors, so's yer Seniory citizens could git land by the river and pass it on over to their sons' and daughters' hairs. Mind you there warn't too many daughters about, so yer Tellon scouts over in France rounded up a buncha girl orfins called yer King's Daughters. They was brung out holesail one winter when it was so cold some batchelors was even thinkin' of gittin' married.

And so they wooden change their minds, Tellon tole 'em

there was a pole tacks on batchelors of ten pounds* a piece... which could run into quite a bit, dependin' how bizzy a batchelor you was.

Natcherly it bein' so cold, the fattest girls got hitched first, but it warn't long before the hole batch got got rid of, 'cause there was a lotta soldiers from the regimen of yer Carryon-Salers who'd bin thinkin' of the girls behind they left. Before you knew it yer entire she-bang was dubbled up to keep warm.

Yessir, Tellon he wanted to raise somethin' else in the place 'sides furs and fish. And he did too: yer habitants of Cuebec growed up from less'n five thousand to more'n five million in jist two hundert year.*

✿ WEIGHTY FEETNOTE

Yer French word fer pound is livre, and you'd be surprised at the number there was of loose livres.

✿ BABY FEETNOTE

Valeda says nowdaze them Cuebeckers rate of childern-baring is lower than enny place in yer West-end wirld. Eggsept mebby West Germny, ware they don't need enny more West Germins on accounta they have a bran new crop of Eest Germins to pervide for.

✳ Yer Voyeurs

Not ev'ry one of them French phesants wanted to git married and keep their feat parrylel to the ground while they raised a few hectors of land by the river with yer coloniac irrigation. There was a buncha pups wanted to raise more'n hectors! They wanted to whoop it up all night long in yer northern bushes and debotch things up with the Injians. I don't think they was out fer more'n a furry canew trip and a darn good time. But them Voyeurs (who much later started their own bus cumpny) without knowin' what they was doin' had made their way acrost North 'Merka uncoverin' most of the continence.

The first of them'd be the young lad worked fer Sam Plain as Chief Boy Scout, Etenny Groolay. Young Et, he was the Great Laker of his time, bein' the first whitey to pass Ureon, Speerier, and Ontaryo altho' you can't blame him fer what happen to Eery.

He was only a tad when he started out, but he never got over playin' Injian. Them aborignals finely got fed up with him one night hard by Lake Simcoe when he was first course on a menyou mainly made up of Cannibal's Soup.

A coupla Three Riverers name of Rattysun and Grossyears got further afeeled into the inferior. They come back to Montreal fuzzy to the gunnels with more skins than Holt Renfrew, but not havin' a huntin' license the French fined 'em both fer bein' gamey and offseason.

Well sir, them two swamp-swingers was so mad they flipped. And they flipped right over to the Anglish side of the fence where they was welcomed as the first French seprators willin' to help skim the cream offa the top of Canda.

✳ Yer Bay Buy

Charlie Eleven* of Angland was the King that Rattysun and Grossyears swung over to. And Charlie yer whatever-his-number was one of yer big givers of mink coats to such chlorines as Nell Grim. Up to then, Charlie and his Nellie had bin kinda board sittin' there on the throne with nothin' partickler on. The year before they'd had yer Great Fire when there was a hot time in the hole town one night, and the year before that was yer Great Pubonic Plaig, which is the old time word fer yer industerearial pollyution. But this year there was nothin' to watch but the meerahs on the sealing. So both yer Monarch and his flour was ready fer some action in furrin' parts.

✻ WRIGGLE FEETNOTE

Valeda claims he was only yer Second, because his Father was the Charles yer First... They always put the King's numbers in yer Roamin' numerals. My gol, what'll them Eyetalians be thinkin' of next?

Charlie got his kid brother, Prince Ruppert, a local peer with a good head, fer to work out the details, and he was the one thunk up the big words on yer charter fer to give'em all a Great Hairy Monopply on yer skin game.✶

Nelly she was all fer it, but yer King was one liked to play the feeled and warn't too keen on the one shot bizness. But when Ruppert and his pals showed him he'd git out of it at least two prize skins from the Beaver lodge, a coupla Elk, and mebbe a Moose or a

✻ FANCY FEETNOTE

"Be it known, buy all these presents, oyeah, oh yeah... Bayday! Bayday!"

Rotarian, he signed up all them Gentlemen Debenturers down to yer Lowest Common Factor. And in return fer yer match pair of beaver 'n elk, all the Gents wanted was Northern Cuebec and Ontaryo, yer Prayery Provinces, and the nice parts of yer North-West Territorials.

They took acrost a nice ketch, yer Nunsotch, and it give them a purty good Hudson Bay sail fer openers. And they soon met a few Injians willin' to unpelt theirselves fer somethin' in exchange and a tiny totter rum.

Well them Bay Days got so poplar, the French hadda git into yer Likker Act too. Yer Voyeurs become delivery-deboys and brung it right to yer wig-warm's door fer a pelt. One of them travailin' salesmen, yer Seer de Lavenderlaundry went so far he porridged his canew clear from Mitchell-a-mackinaw to Lake Winnipeg-eye-oasis.

The hole bizness made yer natives yer middlemen 'tween the French and yer English, and they found it hard to choose, but nowadaze they don't see much to choose between 'em and wood like a distink sassiety of their own.

✳ Yer Frontnack

The French fella what changed the pitcher of things'd be Count yer Frontnack, yer steamed Guvner of Cuebec. But he warn't near so steamed as that High Bishop Level, who kept tryin' fer to git Frontnack to *reggie less alcools,* which means controllin' yer likker.

But yer Frontnackers won out over yer W.R.C.T.U. 'cause church is church but bizness is bizness. And next thing you know, there was a lotta fur-baring Injians that was well hung-over. Yer headquarters of yer furryer trade was Montreal, but Frontnack set up the hindquarters in Ontaryo hard by Kingston. All it was then was yer Fort Catterasstrophy; at that time yer Pen was not yet mitey as yer Sord. But with a wet bar in the Fort, yer early Ontaryo was a place to grow, even if you couldn't stand.

Both sides now, yer French and yer Anglish was determin to git furs frum them Injians without payin' too much fer them. The French used brandy and yer Angles used rum, and between the two of them they sure razed hell with yer Abe-original who in turn razed settledmints up and down yer Sin Lorrent, burning everything in site except a secund morgridge. And if you was in the habitant of livin' in yer rurals, you purty well had to sleep with a fowl piece beside you.

Frontnack bein' paddled

Frontnack found another way 'round them Angled-Sacksons, and that was to Hed West. So he sent out his woods-craftsmen, them bein' fellas who were purty crafty in the woods – what they called in French yer *curios de Boys.*

One of yer more curious curios was Father Hennypenny, a French fryer. He was snoopin' 'round one day hard by yer Queensom Hites when all of a sudden he heard a great roar. Well, yer Hennypenny thought the sky was fallin' before he went 'round the bend and seen yer Nagger Falls. He liked the spot so much, he hung around and started divertin' yer local Injians into bein' Christyans. If he'd gotten them into yer state of holy acrimony he'd bin able to start yer Nagger Falls hunnymoon bizness all the sooner.

Frontnack even sent his gal, La Sal, on the road, but it was that swish-buckler, yer Seer Deeperbill went further and stirred things up the most. He musta bin yer Tom Cruze or yer Patrick Sway-back of his day. He'd be sneakin' a comandoe raid on yer Hudson Bay post facters, even makin' it hot fer them Florider Spanish down Pepsacola way. Then he'd truck over to Norleens fer some snugglin' with Lucy Anna. So by the time Frontnack got thru sendin' out his travailin' salesmen, yer French lilies was blowin' all the way out Thunder Bay way and down to yer Mecksican Golf.

That was when the Eestern Seebored Anglish woke up to the fack that they was bein' slowly but surely encircle-sized. Mind you, yer French thought the Anglish was doin' the same thing to them. So fer a time both sides skulked 'round the other like two picky-pockets in a revolver door.

✳ Yer Repulsion of Yer Excadians

All tolled, there was only a hundert thousand of yer French Canajuns all over, so by goin' down on yer Missysippy they was spreadin' theirselves offal thin even if they had bin laid end to end. Whereas yer New Anglishers was more'n a million and a haff people per square head, and all of 'em stuffed into thirteen unlucky colonists. So somethin's gotta give, as the Department of Wealth and Hellfire sez about the universally of our Meddlycare.

Land was gittin' to be even more poplar than fur by this time and yer Frenchfones and yer Anglican Saxaphones ended up fightin' over it. Yer upshat of them land wars was that the Birtish got back New-fieland and Novy Scotia which was at that time called Excadia.* Now most of the people livin' 'round those parts at that time was French-speakin', and it's kinda frustratin' fer

☼ SHORT-FORMED FEETNOTE

Mainly on accounta the inhibitants was soon to become ex-Canadians.

to conker and then find out there's a lotta forners still livin' there. There was only one thing to do – kick 'em out without so much as a buy-yer-leave.

So yer Halluvagonians come in and asked all them Excadience to swear at them with an Oaf of Yer Legions. Now you take yer av'rage Cape Bertoner he's pretty strick Nitesa Clumbuss and din't wanta change dance halls in midstream. All in all, that evaccinuation was a pretty teeryjerky show.

If youse wanta read the story 'bout it Henry Wordsworth has writ a long fellow of a pome about what went on in yer Minus Basin with one of yer Grand Prey girls called Evaseline. Her boyfriend slipped away from her, and then she was put up fer export too, and neither one of 'em met up till they was both on sociable securities and not able to do much about rekindlin' their sparks.

The main thing to remember 'bout all this was, it was yer Anglish and not yer French what started this Seprator bizness.

✳ Yer Wolf at Yer Back Door

Not all of yer ex-Cadience was took over by yer Anglish. Up in Cape Berton hard by yer Brass Door Locks was this big Fortress called Louieburg. Now don't ask me why a lady fort had a fella's name, but all them Louieburgers was holed up-tite in there and the Birtish couldn't even get at them with their navel blockhead.

'Sides that, yer French had a General, Mucky de Mountclam, who was a snorter of a millytant. And altho' he was outnumbed mebbe umpteen to one, he kept beatin' the Birtish all over. He beat off three Birtish prongs who attacked him hard by Nagger Falls, Tiecountyeryoga, and Ossawaywego, till there was an uproar in yer London Common House.

Yer Birtish Premeer, Will Pit, kept gittin' the blame fer all this from yer Birtish M.P.P.'s. It warn't dreckly his falt, but I guess they all needed a Pit to hiss at. What yer Birtish generals was short on was branes, so Pit permoted a young whippin'-snapper with no chin but a nose that could hoe turnips. Well sir, this young pup (he was part Wolf on his father's side) was give the job of beseechin' Cuebec till they give in.

But yer Guvner of Cuebec was yer Marquest de Vaudeville and he figgered he was impregnant. He evaccinated ev'rybody from the Lower Town and had them all on their Uppers in no time. He brung back yer General Mountclam from the Marrytime farm team, and figgered all they hadda do was hole up in yer Shadow Frontnack till freeze-up, which in Cuebec comes shortly after Laboured Day.

Now below them in yer river was Wolf, and he knew he hadda make his way to the top, if he was gonna git into the histry books. He rented a boat and went up and down yer river after dark with muffled ores.*

✿ WRAPT FEETNOTE

In those days yer nitrates was cheaper.

Wolf was a great reader in scool and had heard 'bout yer Greeks and that Trudgin' Horse. He ast himself what yer Greeks woulda done this time, and that's where he got the idee of goin' in the back way.

Jist upriver from yer Shadow Frontnack-on-the-Rocks was this big crack called yer Wolf's Cave. Wolf he figgered it was a lucky sign to find a crack with his name on it, and he din't care whether there was a real wolfe in that cave or no. He figgered him and his soldyers could heist theirselves up into yer Planes of Abieham.

Jist before they went up yer crack, Wolf resited a piece of memmory work from back in scool:

> Rosaries red, violence blue
> Mornin' glories on yer grave
> I love you.

Wolf said at the time he'd druther of writ that pome than take on Cuebec, but somebody nudged him from behind with a baynet, and up he went.

As soon as him and them Grenadine Gards clum to the top and was in striking distants, they run acrost a few pickets on duty, over-powdered 'em and took away their plack-cards.

When Mountclam led his small farce agin yer Wolfmen, there was a ring-dang-slam-bang battle fer a quarter of an hour but before the end of the first period both captins was morally wounded. Game was called on accounta dark; Mountclam was carried off the field by yer Nurselin Sisters and become amortized and yer Tedium was sung by the quire. Mountclam lost yer battle as well, but them Nurselin nones thought him such a good head they keep it in a glass case even today.

Loan Wolf

As fer yer Wolf, he was give a big send-off post-humorously by Royalty, but I'll bet he'd ruther of had yer royalty from that pome he recit.

✳ Yer After-Mass

The thing what really defeeted Cuebec was the fack that nobody in France give a darn about it. Ev'ry hatterer in Paris was up to hair in beavers and what else was Canda good fer? Yer French King Louie the Next, he was more innerested in yer Lesser Aunt Tillies and ther West Undies.

Yer Paris Piece Treat was co-sined by all sides becuz everybuddy was too tired to play any overtime. All King Louie wanted to keep of us was yer two Newfie aisles of Sam Peeair and Mickey Long. I guess he jist wanted a place where he'd git doody-free cognack and cheap purefumes and that stuff that makes yer heart grow fonder – yer absinth.

So it was yer New French what was left out in the lurch by yer Old French. All them high mucky-mucks in charge got out of Cuebec and took French leave back home: yer Guvner Vaudeville, yer Intended Bigot, and even yer Seer de Levis packed his jeans and ran. That left behind jist yer habitants, yer R.C. church people, and a few seniors.

And who d'you think took charge of the drivin' seat? 'Twarn't yer Birtish conkers, fer none of them could speak yer by-lingo. It was yer Jesyouwait priests acted up as yer inter-middlary and before they got thru, you could go to a Bingo in downtown Montreal any nite of the week.

I guess yer Anglish figgered they wanted the bizness end of yer Cuebec and they din't care too much what them inhibitants does on Sunday.

❊ Yer 'Merken Rising Up

Well, no sooner had the Birtish got yer Frenchies rapped than up sprung all that Yanky hanky panky. Yer King of Angland that time was George yer Hundert and 'Leventh.* I'm not sure what started the ruckus this time, but them Yanks had never got on too well with the Mother's country ever since they was Prodigal Fathers and had to come acrost.* Now they all come over here so's they could warship as they seen fit, and tried to git ev'rybody else to purify God in the same way.

✿ DIENASTY FEETNOTE

Now that don't make no sense to me neither but Valeda says it's a case of Roamin' Noomerals agin. Wish they'd sit still.

Well, by the time George yer three I's got his turn on the thrown, nobody was payin' much attention to him, and most was sendin' parsels thru yer post without stamps. The King he got mad and invited them all to his Royal Party at the Boston Gardens and put tacks in their tea. But Valeda says yer Yanks is all alkyholics-unanimus, so in the middle of the party they all got overbored and threw up ther tea into the harbour.

✿ BUNION'S FEETNOTE

All this is more ackuratly recoded in Yer Pill's Grim Progress.

When George heard about this he was fit to be tied, and the vicey of yer versey too, him bein' madder'n a haddock and spendin' quite a bit of his time at the foolish farm. He got so mad he put his foot down on them Yanks with yer Stamp Tacks, so that by the end of yer fisical year 1776 nobody was even aloud a nickel on the Declaration of yer Dependants.

Well, most of yer Yanks succeeded. They sent George a tellygram what said: "Up *yer* Union, Jack!" and got their own flag made by a little old woman, Bitsey Ross.✶

✿ FAR AND WIDE
FEETNOTE

Later adopted by Congersmen at yer Continental Congers.

Soon's they could, them Congersmen drew up yer Billy Rites, sayin' what they wanted was an open convent freely arrived at. Things got worser in Boston when some demonstraters was hurt at Lexinton and Conkerd, which musta bin one offal bizzy innersection.

Valeda don't b'leeve we should dwell with George Warshinton leavin' Mount Vermin to forge fer himself in the valley and sleep around the hole country till he become yer father of it. She says the only thing as is worth notin' is that the Yank rebellyun tried to git us in Canda to join in their frackass. The funny thing of all is that it was yer Anglishmen in Montreal was the ones willin' to seprate down to yer States. But yer av'rage French-Canadian, him as is s'posed to be loyal only to yer Pope, was the one staid loyal to yer Anglish King! How about that fer yer thought fer the day? I guess it takes all kinds to keep a country together, and that time we was held by yer French connection.

✳ Our Yankys Come Home

✿ INFLATED
FEETNOTE

Valeda tells me yer dollar went a lot further in them days.

Now the Birtish General in all this too-do was yer Lord Cornhaulus – him as lost the toss when Warshinton threw the silver dollar acrost yer Potomack River.✶ The Birtish squares extinguished themselves on yer feeled of battle when they formed up their pantaloons and fell, never to rise agin.

After the Birtish got demobbed by yer rebels and went back home, there was still a buncha Yanks down in yer States that wasn't too pro-Yanky. They was still singin' "God Save Yer King" while the rest-of 'em was standin' up fer "My Country, What's It To Thee?"

Now these pro-Birtish Yanks was called Torees and the main kick yer pro-Yanky Yanks had agin yer Toree was they never did bare arms on yer Merkens side.*

That made them in the eyes of Oncle Sam, nothin' better'n gold brickers and drafty dodges. And they was put thru the mill fer it, lemme tell you. Even if some of 'em was really unconscious objectors, that din't make no never mind to them paterotic Stars and Strippers. Matter of fack, quite a few Torees, 'fore they got over yer Marrytime boarders, was tard and fettered.

✿ MODREN TOREE FEETNOTE

The present encumbrance of Canda, Brine Bullroney is the most pro-Yank Tory I ever seen.

After yer War when yer Congersmen in Phillydelphi brung out yer Billy Rites after their Constitootional, they never said nothin' in it 'bout no am-nasty for yer drafty vaders. So hardly none of them Torees wanted to come back States-side.

So that's how we come to git our first batcha Yanks. And they staid too. There was so many of 'em, they started a hole province of their own, New Brunsick. Up to that time, it was jist a buncha fiddleheads growin' wild.

Even today them old-time Yanks git together and have a meetin' of yer Benighted Umpire Roylists once in a while – a buncha true bloors who still think King George the Hundert and 'Leventh is the cat's peejamas. It's easy to tell yer av'rage Roylist when he's in yer men's washroom at the start of a ball game. He's the one stands up fer yer National Antrum even when his pants is at haff mast.

✸ Yer Upper and Yer Lower, Yer Bertha Two Nations

Some of them Umpire Roylists went even further than becomin' New Brunsickers. They spread theirselves all over yer Atlantic sideboard.

Some crost over to yer Cape Berton and inter-bread with yer High Scotch. Others din't wanta go that far but stopped short in Novy Scotia and become Antigonisticks.*

A buncha yer Roylists went the other way and squattied down hard by Shurebrook in yer Far East Townships. And that's where we run into yer two solltudes livin' side by side and rubbin' eech uther the rong way. That Eestend Township satyri-ist Mortify Richer sez them Roylists was a bunch old reackshunarys who didden wanna mix with yer French cuz they thot they was dissended frum hookers brot over to copulate New France.

Now there's often-times yer French and yer Anglish can't stand each other on accounta they never herd sich langridge. But also with yer Roylist, most of 'em was of yer Anglecan religion and din't wanta go near yer R.C. church which b'leeved in sich things as yer Lost Rites with Extreme Moncton.

To make things worse, over in France they jist had a Revelation of their own and a lotta aristocats who hadn't bin gelatined was comin' out to Cuebec to make more Frenchmen.

Natcherly, this made Cuebec more French than ever, so a lotta yer Benighted Roylists wanted to pick up their belongin's and shuffle back to Buffalo. But most of 'em jist moved to the suburbs west of yer Mount Royl where they come to be called West Mounters. But some moved even further west than Cuebec, all the way from yer Bay of Quinzy down to Sarnya-Winser way.

About this time we also got a big batcha Scotch Persbyteerians who didn't mind yer French churchgoer havin' a place to neel as long as they had a seprate place to stand. That's how the place got divided into two kind of Canadians – yer Upper and yer Lower. It din't mean one was better'n the other 'cause it warn't a case of yer shanty French and yer lace curtin Anglish. In them days nobody had lace curtins and ev'rybody had to use the shanty.

✳ Yer Scotch Come Acrost

It was about yer end of yer ate-teen senchry our country got loaded with Scotch. They flocked over here in drovers 'cause back home in their lairds someone found out you could make more money raisin' sheep than Scotchmen, on accounta you can skin a sheep more'n once.

The first batch was penned up in the hole of a ship and brung over by one of yer overlards, yer Erl of Sellchurch. He brot them Scots here, spread them in klans all acrost our land, till they took us over.*

Yer Hyland klansmen was lookin' fer a

✿ KILTICK
FEETNOTE

Valeda says yer Scotch was took in, not took over. She is low Scotch up to the kilt. She was Valeda Drain that was one of the old Flesherton Drains, but she was a Drain on her father's side, and gits her Scotch from her mother.

nice flat place to curl up fer the winter and swing their stones. So they settled down beside yer Lake Winnipeg-eye-oasis, spread their seed, and started yer Red River serial.

Mackenzie and his matey Scots uncoverin' yer Specific Ocean.

✷ RECURD FEETNOTE

Before Confederation.

✷ BURY-CRATTICK FEETNOTE

Valeda phoned up yer Freedom frum Information bunch in Ottawar to find out what yer "A Mare Usque Ad Mare" meant on yer Canadian Shield, and they told her it was "From Yer CBC," but my gol, them fellas wasn't radio-active in them days.

It was yer Hudson Baystreet sharpers sold them this land, never tellin' them there was already a hole clumpa Crees on it. This led to quite a micks-up. Sometimes yer Scotty got along with yer Cree and sometimes not. When they finely did git friendly, what come outen the hole thing was what they call bein' "Matey." We'll git to that later when they got along worse, 'cause yer riel trubble is yet to come.

Most of yer Scotch was settlers, but there was one or two had the wanderin' foot trubble and went further west to git in on yer Rocky fur trade. One of 'em, Alex Sandy McKinsey, was the first to paddle hisself all the way acrost yer trans-Canda. When he run outta river he'd jist pick up his punt and porridge the prayery.

He got fooled once into goin' too far north by yer Boring Alice hard by Aurora. But he made a fresh start with a fresh chart and with the help of Percy Veerence got all the ways out to Vancoover 1793 B.C.✷

So, Percy Veerence not with standin', it was yer Scotchman found yer cheap charter root acrost Canda from Mare to Mare.✷

✳ Yer Evasion from Yer Eweass

Now that they was two sepratist countries, Canda and yer U.S. of A. started puttin' up boarders and makin' sure each other hadda go thru some strange customs.

But there was some Yanks thought Canda by rites belonged to them. They was a buncha Warshinton Capitolists called yer "War Hocks." They b'leeved in somethin' called "Many-fist Dustiny" which meant that if us Canuckers din't wanta become another star in their flag, they'd roll up their fistick cuffs, dust off their nuckles, and give us a few stripes of our own.

Lorry Seecord (not assorted)

And they meant it. I fergit how the hole offal thing started. Some Yanky gum-boat had a shot-put acrost yer stern of one of our frigits. At the time the rest of yer Royl Navy was all tied up on yer playin' fields of Eaton's agin yer new French upstarter, Napolio Bonuspart. Yer Birtish Jack-in-the-Tar finely beat yer French navvies at Trafalgar Square where they all went down to the Waterloo.

But that was no help to us, left with three thousand mile of fenceless boarders. Mind you, yer Yank high-ups warn't too smart in their stragedy. It woulda bin easy to git sneakers acrost all parts of yer boarder, but yer U.S. general marched bold as his brass acrost yer Piece Bridge and rite up to yer nearest Laura Seacord.

Now Laura she warn't content to sit around like one of yer fanny farmers. As soon as them Yanks set down to eat her outta house and store, she snuck out to the cow barn and decided to pull somethin'. She took out her prize cow, yer local Dairy Queen, and rode it more'n twenty mile barebones. When she got to her General I.

Sick Brock she told him the Yanks was comin' – "over there."*

"Over there" was yer Beaver's Damn now called yer town of Thorhold, but still known by many a visiter as that dam backwater.

Well sir, Brock he jist waited in yer ambushes till them Yanks got to the Hite of yer Queensom hard by yer Hydro. Then he let them have it right in the rear-gard and beat the retreat offa them. Sad to say he got hisself nicked in the frackass when a bullit bounced offa Rick O'Shay and give our General the rigger's morse.

But a greatful country still remembers, and the both of 'em, yer brave Brock and yer fine upstandin' Holsteen farm woman, got to be immoral. And they're both still in bizness today, fer she's a box of choclits and he's a hotel.

There's some Yanks as won't admit it, but when you score up all the fights in that war, it finely come out fer us Canadians, 18-12. After that the States figgerd that the best way to conker Canda was to infilthitrate it with branched plants.

✳ Yer Fur Murge

After we got them Yanks settled in their hash, our Scotchmen started givin' us trubble. Them fuzzy-need curlers all seemed to clan up together, but that don't mean they git along with theirselves. There's two differnt Scotches, yer

Highs and yer Lows, and they like nothin' better than usin' each other as sporrin' partners. Once in a while they'd lay into one another till somebody got kilt.

Out West at that time most of yer Scotch was up to their dirks in fur. They took over yer Montreal fur trait after them French got becalmed by our General Wolf. After yer 18-12 War, no fur-traiters could go down to the States any more lookin' fer pelt. Yer Yank fur don't wear too long anyways, mebbe 'cause the animals had already wore it fer a long time first. But also, the colder she is outside the thicker yer fur, so them clanny Scotch traiters headed north and west. That was right up yer Hudson Baystreeter's alley, and both companies soon found out "two's a crowd."

Red River cart (yer squeaky wheel gits no grease)

But that never stopped yer Northwest Scotch fer when it come to makin' money, them fellas'd cut yer throat behind yer back. Valeda don't b'leeve me, but that's what they done to Lord Sellchurch's Red Riverers, and they was their own flesh and bones – all Scotch and a yard wide. Like I sed, some of them haff-broods was alreddy haff-Scotched. In fack there's still a hole tribe of Scotch Injians called yer McMacs.

But them Matey haffbroods din't know at first what to make of this new bunch of Kilts comin' in to their Red River nomad's land all tartaned-up in their Tammy Chanters. First thing these imported Scotch hylanders done was to put up fences and get the buffalo to shuffle off. Now yer Matey he was never one fer fencin' around; he was purty near allus a gypsee and nowadays he'd probly git arrested fer fragrancy. And as fer yer buffalo, that was his stable food. All them haff-broods needed fer their three squares a day was a coupla pemmy-cans (sorta cold buffalo burgers with razzberry juice fer ketchup).

You seen this happen before in yer old West Holyrood moovy. There's allus two kinds, yer settlers and yer unsettlers – yer wild cattle rusters and yer sheepish bunch. The fack that this time there was some Scotch on both sides din't seem to matter a damsite.

Things got so bad tween yer Mannytober fur-Scotch and yer farm-Scotch, they even had a mass-acker 'tween them. It was hard by a place called Seven-Ups where one day yer uncooler heads pre-veiled. Yer settlers was drawin' lots fer lots when all of a sudden out come yer Mateys rollin' their war-hoops and shoutin' "Scots Wahoo!" Din't take long, but a lotta half-Scots shot lotsa shots at a lotta other Scots, and the only one to come outta this free-assco ahead of the game was the fella cuts the epigrams on yer toomstones.

Yer settler's boss, Erl of Sellchurch, was tryin' to hire some Swish mercy-marys fer to come over and fill a few Matey haff-broods fulla holes. But he was too late. Then he took sick with the TB (or not TB, that's still the question), become fatal ill and woke up one mornin' dead.

Mind you, same thing happen to yer Norwesters the next year. Their Furco went outta bizness when their bank rupted and they went into the hands of yer deceevers. They was took over by Hudson Bay. After the two companies become one joint, ev'rybody become buddy-buddy, like yer Three Mousekyteers – it was one fur all and all fur one.

✳ Rufflin' It in Yer Bush

Well sir, first it was fish and fur, then it was wood and whisky brung in the money. Some of yer first famblys of Uppity Canda was our first booze makers too, them same broors as is now high up in the foreflush of yer cafeteeria sassiety.*

Seems like mosta the trees was chopped down to make barrels for yer stave trade. Then they got filled up with home-brew rotgut, and it was drunk by the same lumberin' jacks chopped down the trees. To git more money fer a bender they hadda go back and cut down more trees, makin' it a kinda viscous sickle of perpetulant emotion.

✿ FOAMY
FEETNOTE

The latest beery news is that the mooseheds in charge of that bizness are gonna git intynashnul Free Trades between the provinces of this country!

It was yer Irish was yer biggest lumberers. They was driven out of yer potato farmin' in Ireland after yer spuds give out. That was when them absentee-minded landlairds from Angland started plantin' Irishmen instead.

So yer Irish steeraged their way over to yer Ottawa Valley and tried to settle down. But the place was already fulla the same kinda starchy Anglishmen had et all their potatoes back home. From then on, there was never any settlin' yer Irish. Ev'ry Saturday night in Arnprior or Carp, it was a ring-tailed snorter of a Highburnyin not-so-fancy-dress brawl.

Moody Susannah

Yer Anglish squire-leaders stuck up their

noses at sich sheenyannigans. One of 'em, a right moody woman, writ a book about how hard it was to be a pieinear lady in them days and wear ruffles in yer bush. Her husband was one of yer Officer's Messes – tryin' to be one of them gentleman farmers can't raise nothin' but their hats. All they ever did was complain, them two; life with them musta bin one long quittin' bee. But *she* griped over farmers what done well, callin' them yer Commoner Man without no edification.*

It was about this time Great-Grandpa Farquharson shipped out here with yer Orange drove from North Ireland. He din't wanta micks with yer left-foot Dogan Irish, so he tried out yer homestead life hard by Lake Simpco. This was a buncha cottiges run by grave John Simpco, Uppity Canda's first left-handed Guvnor.

They was nice people yer Simpcos, but offal name droppers. They even called hole townships after their dogs, Tiny, Floss, Tay, and Matchedash. Valeda's glad they never got no further north or we'd be now likely livin' in Rover or Spot Township.

Now Great-Gramma din't like stayin' 'round those parts 'cause she was a Westly Methadist and the only church there was fer yer Anglecans who was so High they spent mosta their time on their nees. The Farquharsons left when they was told that the only ministers for Method people 'round them parts was yer odd Circus Rider.*

Great Grampa and Gramma moved up Georgian Bay way jist this side of Pointa Barrel. Here they started stumpin' and logrollin'

❁ LONG FEETNOTE

Well my gol, what good has all that Edgy Ryerson book stuff done anyways? What's the use of studyin' up on Animal Husbandry when you know yer stock is goin' to make their own arrangements? Or why try that artifishy insinuation when the cattle prefer draft to the bottled stuff? I tell you the only good thing I got from scool was learnin' to sign my own name, otherwise I'd have to pay cash.

❁ DISTAFFF FEETNOTE

Valeda red in the Benited Church Preserver that sum of them Circus Riders wuz wimmen. She give me sitch a look when I ast if enny of them was bear backs.

and even makin' their own soap. Many's the night they staid up till sunrise smokin' pot-ash. Later they moved to a log house with wall-to-wall floors, which ain't standin' no more but would be now right inside yer Metra-popolitan Parry Sound on the Fourth Concession down by the Town Line not far from the old Orr House.

❈ Yer Fambly Compack and Yer Littlest Rebel

Now yer Compack is not about cars or puttin' on make-up; it's about somethin' else that should be recalled reg'lar. The hole trubble fer farmers today started more'n a hundert years ago when yer city people started pushin' us around.

In our own Province, there was a buncha uppity Canajuns tried that back in '37. (That'd be yer 18, not yer 19.)* In them days, yer local Munipissapill guvmint (that'd be yer Infernal Regional Guvmint) what run Uppity Canda was called yer Fambly Compack. It was headed by Bishop Scrawn, which is spelt SCRACHIN', but you can bet he never hadda do any of that fer a livin', bein' top piller and bolster of yer High Anglecan Church. His aida-camp was John Beverly Robinson, who was anointed Atturky-Genrull and spent his time calling Amerkan immygrunts "aileens" as if they had cum frum another planit. Last and probly least was Sir Francis Blond Head, who soon proved he had nothin' inside it.

✿ BACK FEETNOTE

Yer 1937 was back when a farmer called Mitch Hepburn showed how he knew his onions in polliticks, and he pulled a few other things too.

These three town snobs dumnaynated yer guvermint and grabbed most of yer land fer theirselves what was s'posed to be used fer farmin'. These absenteasers wanted to hold on to their Crown Royl preserves till after us farmin' fools had bilt the place up, then they'd re-zone it to yer city folks at inflammation prices jist as soon as they'd lowered yer real estate boom.

The one sty in the ointment that kept buggin' Yer Family Compack was a little Low Scot name of Willy "The Lion" Mackenzie. When he roared he bugged them city snobs more'n I do my potatos, and he done it mostly by hisself, so you have to give the little bugger credit.*

Willie run what they call yer underground press, and b'leeve me that's where yer right-wing-collared Compack people wished Willy was. They hired some ruff-necks to sneak in one night and throw his tripewriter into Tronto Harbour. Well sir, Willie warn't too ankshus to git out an under-water newspaper, so he run from his office and ended up Hizzoner yer Warship of a shoppin' center called Yorkville, which even then was considered pretty far-out from the rest of Tronto.

But yer Compackers kicked him outen that job too, mainly on accounta Willy din't like their high-rise attitudes and what was gonna develop. They got him band from comin' back into town, and he hadda stay with yer suburbins north of yer Metra-popolitan limits. He spent his time gittin' drunk in Monty Gummery's Tavern, and one day when he was feelin' no pain he thunk up yer Rebellyun agin Uppity Canda.

A buncha other drunks strung along with him, and he mustard all them stragglers down Young Street. They was all three sheets in the wind, havin' made sev'ral stops on the way, and by the time they got hard by yer Make Beleef Gardens, they was in no condition fer a face-off. That was the end of their straggle, fer they was all badly out-numbed and well hung-over. Nobody got hurt or killed tho', 'cause no one fired until they could see the whites of their eyes, which by that time Willy and his fellas din't have any.

You'd think all them High Anglecan Christyans woulda foregave Willy and his revels like they tell you in church. But most of the plodders was driv down to the States and never come back, permamint cross-boarder shoppers.

As fer Willy the Lion, he tried evadin' Canda from the States, but the Yanks put him in jail fer disturbin' yer Piece Bridge, so Willy finely come back to Yorkville and joined yer Established Mint as jist another member of yer House of Assendbilly.

✳ Up Yer Lowers too!

That was quite a year, yer '37 back in yer eighteens. Fer one thing it was the first time old Queen Victorya got put on her throne. It was too bad she hadda have rebiliousness in both her Uppers and her Lowers of Canda.

Yer Lowers had much the same kick as yer Uppers, namely they was gittin' the townspeeples boot up their rurals too. It warn't a matter of yer Frenchy versy yer

Yer Pappynose

Anglish... there was plenty of them on both sides. In fack yer French and yer Anglish farmer has pretty near allus been of the same mind when it come to gittin' the wrong end of yer manoor fork.

The funny thing was yer Church warn't too keen on their phesants gittin' up on their hind legs and demandin' their rites. You'da thought them country people would git some support from their paris priests after goin' to church reglar ev'ry week and payin' their tiths off.*

✿ FISICAL FEETNOTE

Valeda don't like me sayin' that, but that's yer French word fer when they pay ten percent to give Our Lady Perpetyal help.

Funnier still was that it was a city lawyer name of Louie Pappynose (I guess his looks took after his father) what started yer rural balls rollin'. Lou he was already in yer Cuebec guvermint but agin yer Guvermint, sort of a not too loyl Opposite Position. He got all yer French farmers rot up till they bared their arms and sung yer "Mayonnaise."*

✿ MUSICAL-HISTERICAL FEETNOTE

Valeda sez it's yer Martial-aise and they're rewritin' both yer words and yer leericks to make them less bluddy.

That done it. If it's one song yer Cuebecker-in-charge was scared of, it was this one that started that big ruckus in Old France. So yer Guvner suspended Abie's corpus and put Marshal Law in charge of the hole she-bang.

After that, ev'rybody was purty repressed. A lotta yer lefty hot-heads was shipped off to Austria fer to live with yer Kangyroos and Cola bares. (Valeda thinks mebbe it was Australalia where they go down under and wear bathin' soots all winter.) But no matter which, it was still pretty tuff on them French-speakers when even hardly no Anglishmen can understand them Bushymen from down there up under. I hope them Ozzies put a shrimp on the Barbie fer them rebbles.

✳ Yer Loco Motive

After we had them twin rebellyuns, in steereo so to speak, good Queen Victoryus sent out to find what was the matter with us, Lord Durm, one of her best peers.*

Durm, his job was to make a loud report on what to do with our Upper and Lower. Yer Number One Durm recommend was to join up yer French and Anglish into one province and make 'em both responsible fer guvermint. This sure din't tickle yer Frenchie to shout "Who-pee!" since the responsible part

❖ PRIVATE FEETNOTE

Valeda says I din't have to say that and how would I know sich ina-mit things anyways?

meant sharin' each other's detts, and there was already a whopper on yer Uppers.

Number Two also caused quite a bit of it to fly. It was a recommend fer a Rebellyun Lost Bill, fer to constempate them who had lost yer rebellyun and undergone suffrage durin' yer riot acts. This time it was yer lower Canajun Anglish kicked over the traces. Yer West Mounters marched downtown, called yer Guvner Alaclair Fontaine a rotten aig, and started arson 'round yer Place D'Ames. They even started makin' many-fistos and talked about sepratin' down to yer States.

But soon as French customers started spendin' their munny in yer downtown stores, them Anglish merchants got down to bizness, even put sum French on their signs, and took off their U.S. take-over bibs.

Speakin' of fresh capital, Ottawa was chose as the new site fer yer nation's capitalists. Ev'rybody thought it was gonna be Tronto, known in them days as Hogtown on accounta the line-up at the troff. But Ottawa has done purty good since in that department fer a little lumberin' place only noted fer log-rollin' and pork barellin'.✶

Course it warn't called Ottawa up till then. It was bilt by a Newfie named Kernel By, and had been called By-pass. The new name, Ottawa, musta bin out of an old Injian word "Oot-away" meanin' the same thing as yer By-pass.

About this time, two things come around the bend that raised a lotta steam. One was yer railroad train, invented by James What – an old Anglish kettle-man. The other was Sir John Eh Macdonald, an imported Scotch with quite a bite. Them two got together and conceeved berth fer this country.

It's hard to say whether yer coast-to-coast Canda come about 'cause of yer sea-by-sea railroad or the vicey of yer versey. It's a sorta chick-in-yer-aig argument to guess who got laid first.

Mind you, there warn't much layin' goin' on in Canda before this time. Yer States already had five thousand mile of track when us had only fifteen-and-a-haff. But our stock started to roll when Johnny Mac got his first M.P. By the time he got into yer Cabinet (and he was allus in there)

Yer gravy train

they had a railroad named after him, yer Grand Drunk.

It went from Sarnya 'cross yer new suspender bridge at the Falls, all the way up past Montreal to yer Riviera Loop de Loop. Of course yer "Grand Drunk" was jist an old nick's name. Full name was yer Great Western Sandwich and Winser R.R.✶

But there was no railin' in any other part of the country (which wasn't called Canda yet). Yer new dubble province was Canda East and Canda West, and I guess east and west of *them* was jist called "out there." But by gol, there was a heckuva lotta "out there," and it was up fer grabs. If our fellas din't grab it, you know who would!

Us and U.S. had a bounder line, but that only shows on a map. Sir Johnny he wanted a track on record that would be our missin' link-up. He was gonna railrode us into bein' a hole country.

✿ INISHUL
FEETNOTE

R.R. stands for Rural Root, since in them days ev'ry jerkwater got a stop.

Part í yí ☀

❋ Yer Conflergration

It started with yer Charlatan's Confrence, that grate conflergration that was finely put out in 1867. Nobody much wanted it. Yer Marrytimers was up to their arms agin it when their leader Joe How (not Who) told 'em he was sellin' them up the river fer 80¢ a head.

Yer Prince Edward Hylanders never joined up fer another six year, they was so puke-warm about it. My gol, yer Newfie-landers kept their arms folded fer another eighty-two year, and some of 'em still got their fingers crost.

Yer Cuebeckers figgered it was a rip-off to be a minority grope with the rest of yer Anglish popilation. It ain't changed and their guvmint is now bribing them to have less berth controls.✶

Even them Westministers in yer Big Ben's Common House next to the Queen's Privy din't seem to care two-pants about Canda. You take both yer Benjymin Disruly and yer Willy Ewart Gallstone✶ they was

✿ INSENTIVE
FEETNOTE

Rubber Bairasser has bin runnin' a pro-gram called "Kash fer Kids" or "Balling fer Dollars:" five hunnerd bucks fer the first pop, dubble yer munny fer the secund, and if you bang out trippalets you hit yer jackspot fer six thousand. But Cuebeck, it seems, can't be bot. Not fer munny fer luv.

✿ PERSNAL
FEETNOTE

Part of me become named after him. Not his last part but his middlepart, Ewart — pernounced Yurt. Mind, it'd bin closer to the truth to be called Charles Gallstone Farquharson.

too busy tryin' to git in on some of that Yerpeen Free Trade (known nowadays as yer Common Markup).

I think the thing what forced us to git together was probly yer U.S. Sybil War, when yer South-end States succeeded from yer North. That was after John Brown's body got fired from Fort Sumpter.

There was a lotta talk among yer Yanks about startin' up a second front. But about the only ones what tried to come acrost us was a buncha loose Irish Feenymin who evaded us at both ends of Lake Ontaryo – yer Ford Eery and yer Pressedcot. They tried to raise up our I.R.E. but fergot that our little green men was mostly orange.

But the real spirits behind yer Conflegration was pervided by Sir Johnny "Red Label" Macdonald, so let's drink a health to the new country and hope she'll keep goin' rite thru her bi-sextenniel.

The wife she wants to put in a pome which was made up to celibate our 1967 tencenty-all and was give by her, electrocutin' it herself. This here ode is not the first she has writ. Valeda's bin a long-time oder, recitin' at many consorts fer yer Sick and Tired of yer United Church.

ODE ON YOU, O CANDA
(as writ and recit by Valeda Drain Farquharson,
Parry Sound, Ontaryo, July 1st, 1967.)

What is Canda to you?
This land so strong and true.
What does it make you think of,
And why and where and how?
Whenever I think of my country,
It seems like a great big cow.
Yes, a Guernsey or a Holsteen,
Is that sich a foolish notion?
Lappin' its fill of the waters

Of our very own Pasifick Ocean.
Then chewin' its cud on the Prayerees,
Right over yer Kickin' Horse Pass
In the breadbasket of our nation,
As it regurgitates its grass.
And settles its mash in Ontaryo,
Where its udders gently sway sweet,
Waitin' fer stockbrokers to milk it,
Down there on old Bay Street.
Then to the loins of our country,
Where somethin' surely is stirrin'!
Listen and you can hear
A rumblin' and grumblin' and whirrin'.
The wind of change is blowin'!
Can't you hear its howls?
As we wonder at all those movements
Deep in our nation's bowels.
And so we come to the end of my tail
And all its little rimes...
And doesn't this allus happen
To the dear old Marrytimes?

✳ Yer Red River Serial (First Riel)

We was only four provinces first off, but you take yer Sir Johnny Macdonald he was allus ready fer a fifth. He got worried about the soft underbelly of our breadbasket when a lotta Yanks started infilteratin' up our flanks and squattyin' on yer Winnypeg must-keg.

This was up in yer Norwester Terrytoryals where yer Hudson Bay was still a big facter. They din't seem to mind forners comin' up from yer south, but they warn't too keen on farmers comin' in from yer east. A lotta them farmers decided to git rid of yer Bay Boys and filed their partition up to Ottawa fer to have a big Hudson Bay Sale.

Upshat of it was a good deal was made of it on both sides. Yer Bay skint the guvermint fer a lotta money, and us farmers got another province, called then by an Irish name of yer Asinnerboyo but changed by more sober Orangemen to Manytoper. The only ones left out on the deal was yer Injian and yer Matey, yer cold prayery's original residents.

Nobody bothered to tell them there was a new province where the deer and the antelope pay.

Them Matey Injians begun to hear a discurragin' word when surveyors started to pull the chain acrost their strip farms.* Turns out them plum-bobbers was surveyin' ahead of theirselves. Yer Hudson's Bayers had moved out, but Ottawa hadn't yet moved in, so ev'rybody was jist hooverin' around in a vackyume.

✿ PINK
FEETNOTE

Valeda din't want me to find out about that kinda Dukeabhor aggerculture. She says you don't have to be indecent to make a bare livin'. And all that arson around don't help neether.

Up jumps a smart haff-brooder name of Louie Riel, starts to run the vackyume and clean up fer his own people. Louie he'd bin purty near a priest but jist missed takin' orders. Sure loved to give them tho'. He and his Mates took over the Fort Garry Hotel and roust Guvner McDoogle outta his room and private bath.

Things started to happen. Bishop Sashay got recalled from the Vaticacan fer to try some of his divine intravention. Donald Smith was sent out with a bag of money by Ottawa but couldn't git a room at the Fort Garry 'cause they din't b'leeve it was his real name. He changed it to Lord Strathacorona and they even put up his horse.

Yer newest Father
of Conflergration
(Fer Riel!)

But one fella, Tom Scot of the Orange Lodge, jist sassed Louie somethin' offal. Louie put him in the cooler but he kept gittin' hotter, so the hot Scot got shot. Well sir, that sure started things off with a bang and we ain't heard the end of it yet. You could write off the next hundert years by the smoke from that one shell. Troops of Orangemen was sent out, Louie become a fidgetive from yer just sassiety, and a lot of his Mateys got knocked off.

That was the end of yer first Riel, and more to come. The reason give fer all them bullits was one fella was a Orangeman and the other was R.C. But my gol, that ain't what it was about atall. It was about pullin' yer chain over another man's land without a buy-yer-leave. Any workin' man knows how that feels when the new highway or the new high-rise condominimum goes thru.

If that Riel bullit had hit anuther Cathlick you might never have heard any more about it. But we did. We're still heering about it. Louie Riel has jist bin unhung by the same Torys that got him hung-up in the first place. Once thot to be mad, he is now offishully Manytober's only livid Father of Confedration.

✳ Off Yer Rail

Now that them Red Riverers was settled down and startin' to call each other Manytoberers, old Johnny Macdonald was thinkin' of stretchin' our bellyband again. By this time Birtish Clumbia was makin' sheepish eyes his way, mainly on accounta their last year's Gold Rush had peter out.

The town they'd bilt speshully fer minors had gone to the dogs (which is why it's now called Barkervill) and you even hadda watch yer step on that Carrypoo Trail. But yer B.C.'s was waitin' fer somethin' else with steam risin' from it to be comin' 'round yer mountin', and when she come, that's when they'd sign in as Number Six.

So Sir Johnny he set out to raise some capitolists. But to show them Victorians and New Westministers he wasn't foolin' he give a fella name of Sendfer Phleming his walkin' papers fer to lay everythin' he could on a map, so's they'd be ready to start bildin' accordion to his blue-points.

It was easy to git started on paper, but harder to raise yer rail. Money that time was titer'n a bull's arsehole in fly-time.* Some of the Grits thunk Sir Johnny shoulda riz up the money from yer public sextors 'stead of scratchin' around his privates. But due to yer

✿ SORE FEETNOTE

Valeda got madder'n a set hen when I got this one out. She feels I shoulda used the plite word fer it, which is yer animal, not yer bull.

56 ✿

Recent Prostity Treaty, yer tarf was already purty high on deported goods without addin' no Exercise Tacks, either pervinshul or G.S.T.＊

☼ OVERTAXED FEETNOTE

The ladder wasn't added till lader. Its inishuls stand fer "Gittin' Scrood Twice."

But our John finely got a tite wadda money from a buncha Canuck sindycats had made their piles in the U.S. Turned out they'd made it railroadin' too. One sure way to git to be a malted millyonair in them days was to be in yer railroad supply bizness and git yerself a contrack fer to bild an R.R. Then you'd sell yerself all the stuff you said you needed at yer own price. It was better'n gold-brickin' or counter-feetin'. Don't think yer guvermint M.P.'s din't git in on the racket too, formin' their own companies and sell-in' track to you and me from their own backyards. Now that's what you'd call a public trussed.

Well, when he got the money, Sir John he started burnin' it at both ends. He had two track teams workin' each coast and layin' fer each other till they met in the middle. Accordin' to Phleming's map that shoulda bin about Moosejaw, but one of yer teams made a pass thru yer Yellahead thru yer Rocky and the other fellas got micksed up in

Sir John, eh?

yer Kickin' Horse's Ass and come out way below yer Moosejaw, about yer Moose'snee.

When the neither of them met, they both kept on trackin' to the other end of yer country, and that's why today we got two railroads, yer C.N. and yer C.P.

Them two sets of trackers had hardly took off their ties and got down to work when there was an offal stink in yer

Common House lit by this specifick scandle. Turns out Johnny Macdonald had bin gittin' a little more grease from them big railroad wheels than we all knew about.

A vote was took. There was a lotta no-confidence men agin him so him and his party was railroaded outta office, and Sir Johnny's pet projeck was stop ded in its tracks.

✴ Yer Rail On

Well sir, after old Johnny Macdonald's chickens come home to the rooster, he slipped under the table to become Leader of yer Opposite Position. His place as Primer Minister was took over by Alex Sandy MacKinsey, a stoned Mason. As head of yer Common House he turned out to be a block offa the old chip. Fer four years he sat there stiff and stately, hardly movin' atall jist like yer av'rage statute.

Meantime yer coastercoast railroad got rustier'n the bottom of my '58 Edsel.*

✿ ANTEEK FEETNOTE

Now obscolene. Yer Edsel looked like a Ford car chasin' a tilet seat.

But there was Johnny (Mickdonald) left standin' in the roundhouse without a corner to hiss in. He got his steam up next 'leckshun, and was back on the old stumpin' grounds tellin' ev'rybody to exorcise their french-fries on his b-haff.

They done it too. Them Torees got back in quicker'n Pee-Air Terdo on his secund cumming. And the first thing Sir John done was mount a few soldyers and start up them musical riders yer R.C.M.P.'s.

Seems a buncha Yanky bootyleggers had bin crossin' the boarder into Alberto and cheatin' our Injians outta their furs by givin' them bad likker. Ev'rybody was so sick of them rennygades doin' this, they called the place where they done it Fort Whoopup. Well sir, it wasn't too long before our Mounted Redcaps got a half-nelson eddy on them U.S. boozehounds. The bootleckers skeedaddled acrost yer Mount Anna boarder and never showed theirselves up our way agin till they got back in bizness in yer 1920s when Warshinton legallyized Inhibition.*

Second thing on old Johnny Macdonald's list was makin' tracks fer the west coast with his C.P.R.R. To git the job done Sir John hired hisself a Yank who ended up livin' in Canda. His name was Van Horen and he was a ring-tailed snorter of a billy-goad. He smoked like a steaminjun, drank like a dubble boiler, and swore like a conductor with a hot box. But he was a reel driver, and he got the hole she-banger laid in haff the time she was to of took.

✿ DRY FEETNOTE

Valeda claims all that Inhibition was done mostly by the good work of yer W.C. to you.

The only trubble at yer Common House end was razin' all the cash. Old Sir Johnny was floatin' lones and waterin' the stock till he was up to his armed-pits in sudsities. But he knew there was only two things would hold this country together: a railroad, and the fack that ev'rybody else hates Tronto. But purty soon it got to be a case of whither a railroad was goin' to run acrost yer hole country, or yer country was goin' to be run into yer hole in the ground.

This pit Sir John into a kinda deepression, as well as keepin' him on the horns of a dillenema. But he got offa his horns when Louie yer Riel come back from States-side where he'd bin spendin' his part time teachin' scool and his other part bein' inmated in a funnyhouse.*

✿ TWISTED FEETNOTE

Valeda says from what she's heard about yer Yank scoolin', it was probly the other way 'round.

Seems Louie was assed back here by his Mateys who was bothered by the railroad-bildin' which was makin' it hard fer them to cross over the tracks and hunt up their Buffalo connections. So they had joined up with the Big Three of yer Injian Cheefs – Big Bare, Crowsfeet, and Poundcaker.*

Crowsfeet he finely pulled out 'cause he din't like the new wrinkle they was plannin' to pull, namely yer White Massa Cree.

Well sir, if it was yer railroad started this haff-brood trubble, it was yer railroad finished it in short orders. Sir John was able to rush troops under General Middleman flat in no time by rails. They carried him out hard by Saskytune with his rattlin' Gat gun, but mind you, even with all that he never done too good agin yer Matey leader, Gabe Dupont.

Gabe he was a man of a few words, mainly on accounta he never learned to read nor wrote, but my gol, you stand him on the next concession and he could shoot the tips offa yer bull. Him and his little buncha Matey irregular gorillas purty near beat the retreat offa all them Reglar Army Malicious.

But fired-power will out and it warn't too long before them poor Mateys was surrounded up. Gabe Dupont lit out fer the States and ended up as a sharkshooter with Annie Oakvill in Wild Billy Cody's Three-Ring Bulls-eye Show. As fer the Riel leader, Louie got arrested in his development and tried fer sev'ral treasons. They finely tied the knot on him nine days after yer last spike was driv up Craig's Alley-key to finish off yer C.P.R.*

☼ KNOTTY
FEETNOTE

Some Orange people still claims he was jist as well hung. Valeda says it don't matter what they did to him, you can't call it tyin' the knot which only refers to yer state of holy acrimony. Myself I think she's out of it, fer nowadays when a young couple talks about tyin' their knot, they're more 'n likely talkin' about yer Vasextummy.

Ever since then, most of yer land-claims of yer indigent naytif peoples has bin ignore with the guvmint's undivide attention. But this issyuh won't go way. Sure as shootin'.

✸ Yer Poet Lorry eh?

When Sir Johnny Macdonald finely passed on to yer Great Conservatory-in-the-Sky, his place was took by a purty old man, Mackenzees Bowel, who had trubble gittin' people innerested in any of the movements he placed on the floor of yer House.

So come next election, yer Tories was out, and we was handed a brand new bag of Grits under a fella had a silver tongue to match his long lox. You mind Sir Wilful Lorry, eh? He sure cut a poetical figger, in his candyfloss hair and his frog-tailed coat. When he went over fer yer old Queen of Victoria's dymondjewbilly, he struck her so fancy she ast to have him nightied.

Mind you, he was pretty frale in health ever since he become leader, when the mantle fell on him at a grate Libral party. But don't let that fool you, fer beneath that velvet coat there was a iron ham in it, and he could act like a reg'lar automat.

One of the things he went right to work and done was to settle up yer West. Ever since yer second Riel fit had been fot, most folks was scared to live out there fer fear of gittin' tommyhocks in their backyard. But Sir Wilf he told his Minister fer Yer Inteerier to put adds in the newspapers all over yer world, advertizin' "The West, A Nest, and Ewe." And by gol, if a lotta sheepish farmers din't turn up from as far-away as yer Ukerain, some Dukeabhors from behind yer Rurals, and they even got a herd of Crotes and Surbs by the Balkin's. Before too long, ev'rybody was bustin' their sods to set up a homin'stead, and we had us two new Prayery providences before you could say Don Massacowshitsky.

Another thing Wilf done was to set up yer Penny Post Office under yer General Pastmaster, Sir Willyam Mule-Ox.

Right away it got to be more poplar than "Snakes'n Ladders." Before Christmas they hadda dubble their staff in Ottawa. Yessir, hadda have the two of 'em there, one fer settin' and sortin', the other fer standin' and handin'. Now it's all auty-o-mated, and lotsa lokel post-offices is goin' thru a prosess of elimination. Up our way we don't bother no more. We jist hand our mail to Them Jehova's Witlessess; they're going door-to-door anyways.

Lorry, eh? – a bust

One thing Sir Wilf got mixed up in he mebbe wisht he hadn'ta was yer Boor War. This hole thing started when some of yer bigger Boors refused to let an Anglishwoman, Lady Smith, use one of their public conveenyances which was sedgeregated on accounta in yer South of Afrike they don't use nothin' but yer apart-heads. Well sir, it took an offal lotta troops from all over yer Umpire to make sure that Lady Smith got releeved, and before it was all over some of our boys had a hand in it.

Wilf also give Canda its first navy, called yer "Tinpot Navy," meanin' it really wasn't much. Yer Canadian Admirables was all give shore duty at yer Royl Navel Hospitable where they was aloud to be in charge of all yer vessels under the beds. Wilf got in trubble from all sides fer this. Yer Cuebeckers thought he was actin' too Anglish, and the rest of us thought he was regurgitatin' back to bein' a darn fool Frenchman. Ackshully, it was a case of six of one and a haff a case of the other. But this same sorta thing happens today. We gotta Prime Minster rite now, Brine Baloney, who is offen accuse of bein' more Frenched than Anglished, witch tends to git his Ire-ish up.

Lookin' back on his speeches, there was one other thing Sir Wilf was wrong about. He's the one what said: "Yer Twentieth-Century belongs to Canda." I think if you'll check the books, 'speshully the bankbooks, you'll find out yer Twentieth-Century belonged to Fox.

✳ Yer Kyzer Rolls

King Edward yer Seven was the first outta Victoria by Albert, so he sat on his mother's throne when she got finished. He soon become known as yer "Playboy King" with his big centre spread. He finely got laid by yer West Minister's Abby and all of the kings of Yerp come to his last confinement. There was Kyzer Billy of Germany, yer Zar Nickelass of Roosia, and Fran's Josef, yer Impurer of Australia-Hungry.

Funny thing was that all them fellas was kissin' cuzzins, and jist four years later they was all Grate Warrin' with each other. And I don't mean jist a fambly drunk-up on a Sardy night; I mean a more 'n four year bash what got the hole world in a mess.

I'm not too sure what started the hole thing off; I think Fran's Josef got his hair assassinated somewheres in Suburbia.* But Kyzer Billy-B. Dam was jist itchin' fer a fight

✧ UPDAIT
FEETNOTE

Ackshully it was Sairy JayVoe, berthplace of liddle Meal-a Pivnitky who becum a Mulruiny and our First Lady (giver take a Mizz R.H. Natyshn).

anyways, him and his Chief Staff and Comfort, Vaughan Hinderburger, better known as "old bloodied guts."

The reason them high mucky-mucks in Yerp got into conflick was 'cause they was allus playin' alleys. Yer French was alleyed up with yer Roosians, and yer Germins was tradin' dibs with yer Oster-Hunkies. But come 1914, these boys was playin' fer keeps.

Now you'll wonder how Canda got drug into all of this, but at that time she done whatever yer Birtish said, and accordin' to some kinda Boner Law yer Birtish was alleys with little Bellygum.*

So when yer Kyzer rolled acrost that Bellygum, that set Canda right up beside the alleys, which meant our best young men hadda go off by theirselves fer four years. Most of our country thought it was a paterotic thing to do, but there was two bunches din't agree. One was yer French Canucks and the other was yer farmers all over. They both wanted the young fellas to stay at home and git in the hay. I can't say as I blame them, fer this hole World War Part One shoulda never took place. If all us workin' people had mebbe struck out and lay down on the job, them crowned potentaters of Yerp mighta hadda do the fightin' theirselves. You can bet there'da bin no contest.

Mind you, once our boys was in, they sure felt their presents. They extinguished themselves at places like Eep, Passiondale, and Shimmy Ridge. Some of 'em was even up in the air with yer Royl Flyin' Corpse. One of these boys, a bishop from Owen Sound, shot the aces offa seventy-two Huns over yer Red Barrens.

A lotta our rejmints come outta that war covered in, 'sides other things, glory. Their names are Legion, and you'll probly find them at the back of the hall. But to name jist a few, there was yer Tronto Scotties, yer Princess Patties, yer Vin Douce (they was a Cuebec rejmint used to carry sweet wine in their water bottles), and them Montreal Ladees from Hadees, yer Black Watches. I guess yer Germin calvary had never seen fellas draggin' acrost nomads land in skirts before, and when they shouted their war cry, "Dior Go Bra," them Jerry horses jist reared up and all you could see was a clouda horeshat and small stones.

Well, it's all over now, and ev'ry November 11, we shut up fer two minutes jist to perpetuate yer Grate War and buy a poppy fer them as dyed in vein. But by gol, if that was the war to end wars we coulda done without it, includin' yer Treat of Versehigh and yer Leega Nation.

Twenty year later, the hole rang-dang-doo come up agin, and agin our best young fellas left their bones bleachin' behind them. Valeda thinks the next war should be fought in Absentya, wherever that is.

✸ Yer Next to Last Post

When yer first post war finely come, we was all under Sir Robert Boredem and his Coal-Issue guvermint. Sir Robert he give over the seals in his office to Arthur Me-in, 'cause he wanted to retire to stud with his wife Elsie, yer Lady Boredem.

But it was time fer the country to go to the Poles, and when yer returns was in, Me-in was out. It was a new start-up name of Mackenzie King assended his way to power. And he staid there fer the next three decadents, give or take an R.B. Benny.

Boredem

One reason we had a King so long was, he was the only man in Canda had the trick of sittin' on the fence and at the same time keepin' his ear to the ground. He warn't a tall man neither, altho' that statute they put to him outside yer Common House must be purty near nine feet tall, but you know how them Grits tend to eggs-aggregate.

Durin' yer War, King he'd bin down in yer States in labour, which is mebbe why he wasn't prescripted fer the Army. He come back here to be a sybil servant but finely got elected into his office after bein' ejected a coupla times and even once blowin' his deposit. But once he was in, he staid in fer morn a quarter of a centurion.

When it come to gittin' down to bizness King he b'leeved more 'n less in yer *lazy fairy*.[11] But a buncha Westerners was gittin' tired of bein' the sandwich 'tween yer Eastern profitears and yer Ottawa frate rates. So they got up a party of their own and call it One Big Union. This never caught on much back East, partly 'cause in French it comes out like Une Beeg Onion, and the other partly 'cause yer Ontaryo farmer was already united in yer U.F.O. which had nothin' to do with yer unindemnifiable flying objecks.

❁ BY-LINGAMAL
FEETNOTE

This jist means "keep yer hands offa my bizness."

Some mettle workers in Winnypeg went even further out. They'd heard about yer Roosian Evolution got up by yer Marks Brothers, Tropsy, and Lemin, and they figgered they could try the same kinda Bullshyvism at yer Porridge and Main. All they did was sit on their rights fer a six week general strikeout, but the way them Mounties rid their horses agin them, you'da thought they had decomposed King Mackenzie and had him abdicatered. I know yer R.C.M.P.'s allus gits their man, but did they have to go after their women and childern too?[12]

❁ RED
FEETNOTE

Valeda don't think it was our Mounties coulda shoved them people around. Mebbe it was the horse's asses over 'em.

But none of this uprest ever got nowheres. That sly little King, he jist smiled like a Chest-hire Cat and talked a lotta garbiage till nobody knew where they was at, 'cept him. I think the only time anybody ever heard that man commit hisself out loud was the time he patted his dog and said: "It's a bitch."

The King and
the once and future Pat

One good thing that happen durin' his rain about this time was at yer Best-Banty Instantoot where they found out you don't have to die a suger-beetis if you have enuff Insolence. Them fellas got the Noble Prize fer this, and Valeda's kinda sorry they din't git medals from Parry Sound and Mactier as well.

Another bit of culture that come up was yer Grope of Seven – a buncha drawers clustered together and went around the north country paintin' barns and outbildin's by the numbers. But fer my kinds of culture – yer horti and yer agri – it was yer boom and yer bust. Wheat'd be two dollars yer bushel one year and a dollar fer two the next. All yer av'rage farmer'd git fer his sweat haff the time was a little Pool of Wheat. But then in yer mid-Twenties, yer boom stuck fer years and ev'rybody figgered posterity was around the corner. Yer Farmers' Movements petered theirselves out, and about the only thing really lasted was the women gittin' over their suffrage, becumming persons, and bein' able to vote or go to their reward in the Canadian Senate. Now they're tryna git Eekwall pay fer work of Eekwal volyume and are about reddy to stand up in the Men's Rooms fer their rights.

But rights or lefts, it din't matter in '29 when them broker fellas on Wall Street told us all their bottoms had fell out.

❋ Yer Dip Depressyun

Yer Big Crash of yer Ded Stock Market (as oppose to our Live Stock Market) sure put a crimp in the 1930s meetin's of our Parry Sound Progress Club. There was even talk of turnin' yer Pomp-payin' Room of our Brunswick Hotel into a soup kitchen. Many a man 'round our concession was all fer pullin' outta his small-holder to move down to Tronto and join them urbane unemployables on the Pogey.

But us mixed-up farmers had a better time of it than them one-a-croppers out West.

Wheat was gittin' 38¢ the bushel, but thru yer lien years of yer drout hardly no crap atall was up-comin' outta the ground. Fer five year – that'd be yer '33 to '37 – yer hole West was dryer'n a grasshopper's talebone. When yer rain did come finely, it come down solid, and all them poor Westerners could croak was: "Gang, Gang! The hail's all here!"

Yer choice wheats that year was yer No. 1 Rusty and yer No. 2 Smutty. You'd think Ottawa woulda tried to help ev'rybody, but there was a lotta conflick 'tween yer Pervincials and yer Dumbminions. King Mackenzie he sat on his fence and said he'd be gosh-darned if he'd give a nickel to any outta-workers under a Tory Pervincial Premeer. Well, after he said that, I wouldn'a give a nickel fer his chances in the 'lection. And sure as hootin' yer R.B. Benny fit in and King was out with his dumb minions.

Now it's hard to say whether we all voted fer R.B. yer Sundy Scool teacher or R.B. yer millyonair lawyer. Myself I think it was yer comby-nations of yer both, most people bein' curious as to how a fella could be the two things at once.

R.B. figgered if he couldn't raise the wheat, the least he could do was raise the tarfs. I think on that one he shoulda checked with yer exports. There was nothin' goin' outta the country and nothin' comin' in. Yer bizness cycles was in yer state of suspended con-stipation.

A buncha unemployds out on yer West Coast tried to steal a march on Ottawa, but only got as far as Regina where they was met with many-fistos per-vided by yer R.C.M.P. The big Boy Scouters was still out to git their man even if he din't have a job.

Up to that time we was all in Canda either Toree or Grit. But people out West had got so fed up with not bein' fed, they up and threw some parties of their own. Yer C.C.M. was a veehicle thunk up by a

Arby Bennet (He got all the beefs)

church minster, J.S. Woolworth, and yer Sociable Crediters was drummed up by Bible Bill A.B. Hart. He was one of yer Prayery Evangels was allus seein' pie in the sky, and promisin' ev'rybody a cut.

Down-and-out Cuebeckers wanted to have a party and Morris Duplenish was jist the fella to give it to 'em. He give it to 'em good fer twenty year, but not so good as he took, which was Duplenty. So much that he finely hadda pass a Padlock Law fer his piggy bank.

The Depressyun was hardly felt by yer Marrytimes 'cause they thought it was s'posed to be like that. But out in Newfieland they hadda be baled out by Grate Breton. She took over the hole island in '33 – hook, line, and sunker. And people was so depressed there was nary a sound of protest, 'cept fer the odd Screech.

Mind you, ten year later Newfieland was a-boomin'! And so was yer Western pandhandlers! Why? 'Cause yer war guns was a-boomin' too. Seems like ev'rytime they stop makin' a killin' on yer Stock Market and go into a Dip Depressyun, the only way man's kind gits out of it is by makin' a killin' on each other. Yer Homely Sapio is allways workin' to make hisself an ex-stink sassiety.

❋ Yer Second Whirl at War

You take yer av'rage war, it's an offal price to pay fer gittin' out of a bizness slump and into yer holycost. There warn't so many uniform fellas knocked off as in yer '14-'18 ruckus, but a turble lotta plainclothes people was. Fifty millyun. This kinda post-naval berth control is cuttin' off yer nose to spike yer drink.

How it started was yer Germin, yer Eyetalian, and yer Jap all had Axes 'tween them. Yer Germin started first, stuck his nose into Pole-land. The first six months or so was called yer "phoney war," 'cause nothin' really happened; both sides was jist phonin' it in behind their lines.

But all that stopped when Germins bliss-creaked their way into them Netherglands. After that yer Eyetalian dicktater Mussel Eeny stabbed someone's back in France, and yer Axes was in.

Yer Birtish hadda evaccinate theirselves hard by Dumcurk, and Bungle fer Briton. That's when Nevey Chamberlinen folded like his umbrella. In come Winsome Churchhill to give us yer two fingers up and told yer Naztys to bring on their Pansy Divisions. But my gol, they never come. Twenty miles of Chanel and they never set a goosed foot on yer White Cleft Dover.

Her man Goring thought he'd conker by airmales. He ordered yer Berlitz on London and his Lustwafflers kept droppin' bums over St. Pall's and other sites fer sore eyes. But when we sent up a few Spittlefires, them Germin Junkies went scurvyin' back to ther Fodderland.*

Well sir, after yer Big Berlitz come yer Long Sitz. Ev'rybody sat around on the end of the Lendleash.

Next thing that happen was way out in yer High-wayin' Islands hard by Honeylooloo – a buncha Bananzy Japanee pilots committed Mata Harry on yer U.S. Navel. This wuz a dirty trick, and so was what we dun to our own Canadian Japanee right after, most of hoom was Vancoover-born, had never even seen yer Nipon. Jist the same they wuz round up, confistificated of their homes and sent deep into Canada to be inturd. They got hassled fer been Orientail-lookin rite up till 1949, and a lotta maid-in-Canda Japanee got compulsivly repastryated to Japan after the war. As fur them as staid heer, they never went back to ther old homesteds, and it tuck anuther farty yeers fer to git any fine-anshul remooneration.

But that was like yer Club Mad compair to what Impurer Shapiro-Hito's farces dun to our Canajun boys what was took prisner after the fall of Honky Dong. There wernt no Ginheaver Convenshun bein' held out there in yer Fur East, and them Rising Suns of you-know-what got away with, in some cases, merder.

Them of our boys as cum back was mostly incapassitated. They got apollojeez frum yer Impeerious Japan, but they're still waitin' fer propper Workin' Condensation.

> ✿ FLYIN'
> FEETNOTE
>
> Valeda says how could them Germins teach Junkies fer to fly. I told her it was jist the names of their airplanes, and now she won't let me mention them other Fokkers and Messyschitz.

Canda was the first of our alleys to open a second Frunt. It was called yer All-Can Hyway, named after the number of beer containers throwed out by soljers and civilly-un bull-dosers and all them mother truckers who drank their way from Dowsin to Farebanks. They bilt it at the rate of 8 mile (or sex hunnerd beer cans) a day. A lotta them workers was Marmtimers witch is why the most common cry out on yer musky-keg when them bulldoser blaids was crackin' with the cold like glass-pains was "Lard Tundra Jeeziz!" Nobody's sure wether it was bilt to stop yer Japaknees frum evading us durin' the war or to skeer off yer Roosians after the war. She's jist had her golden analversry, and long may she be maintained and macadamized.

✳ Time Fer a Peece

After V.D. day, witch ment Vickery in Yerp, everybuddy now tern ther attenshun to Ayzure. We expeckted to go hoppin' frum Island to Island till we reech Toke-yoe, and everybuddy figgered it to be a long hall. But our alleys had a tricker two up ther sleaves, lerned partly frum that capchured Germin rockit star, Wormer Vun Brawn. Unnoan to us, Wormy and our boys had bin doin' some nukuler fishin' on the side. They split a Addem between 'em and got off a cuppla atomical bums, witch they axploded during a candle-stein exspearmint in yer New Mexican's dessert. That was yer outta town openin'. Then they tride them out on yer Japanee maneland hard by Hero-sheeny and Yoke-a-homo.

That end up Wirld War Eleven with a bang, but ther was more than a wimper about dropping sitch a lode of radio-action on a buncha ornery peeple without arms. Yule notice that nobuddy has tride sitch a thing since. (Crotch yer fingers and hope not to die!)

But them 2 nookyler bums sure made peece brake out fast. Before ya knew it, everybuddy was celibating D-J Day, eggsept in Hallyfacks ware they put the damp on our navel's spearits by lockin' up the licker stores. Lemme tell yuh, the goin's on THAT day was a absalute rye-ut, more like the start of Wirld War Three.

Lookin' back now, it seems like our former enemas has figgered out other ways to conker besides yer millinery digressions. Japan is doin' so much better now with their Grater East Azure Co-Posterity Sfear selling Sonys and Panda Sonicks. Same fer Jermny until they broke down that wall and let their eastern poor nabers of yer all-Wellfare state join their pogey.

Old-timers hoo'd bin around at the end of Wirld War Eye was all set fur anuther deep depression now that the peecemungers were havin' ther day. But post-war posterity was jist around the corner. Now that they had lost their war footing, the Grit guvmint up to Ottawar figgered they better have a peece progrum to catch some votes. They opted fer a new twist that had worked before in the durty thurtys, U.S. Precedent Frankie Roseyfel'ts Nude Deel.✳ Canda was about to go frum a warfare to a wellfare state. Even the Tories cot the wind of all this and changed their name to yer Regressive Preservative party.

Fer Canajuns who never got overseized, this war had ment nuthin much more than garnteed employmint and a cuppla rashin

✿ SOILED
FEETNOTE

Valeda sez the turm durty 30's was used by that P.R. Berton in his book about his deep depressyun. Both Valeda and I remember that the only smut around at that time was on the wheet.

books (meet and gass). We ree-cycled back in them days too, long before the guvmint got us by our Bloo Boxes. We kept saving all kinds of scrap and crap fur the wore effurt, and wives even renderd ther lard and drippins back to the butcher.*

❂ CAFF'S
FEETNOTE

I mind a sign in our
lokel carnyvore store:
LADIES DON'T BRING YOUR
FAT CANS IN HERE ON
WEAK ENDS!

The wimmen probly dun this on ther way in to work at the armymint plant. That was the biggest change on yer hoamfrunt – the fack that wimmen didden stay home wile ther men was at the frunt, but went out to work, doin' ther bit and gittin' well-pade fer it. Our country was self-defishunt in them days, speshully in the first cuppla yeers of the wore, when the States was not in on it, but staid nooterd. We was on our own fer probly the last time in histry. There wernt no nashnulized banker like John Crow in them days borryin' munny frum some forner to pay off the intrust on our defickit. We riz all the doe fer that big conflick by borrying frum arselfs with Vickery Bonds.

Mind you, by the time peece cum, accorn to the sadisticks, seventy purrsent of forn investmint in Canda was frum yer Ewe Ass, ware before it had bin Briddish. That's probly cuz the fella in charge of our Wore Effurt was a Yank hisself, Seedy How. He manedge to tock Canajun biznessmen into workin' fer him up to Ottawar fer only a doller a yeer. (That's probly the last time us taxpayers got value fer our money.) When them doller-yeerers went back home to settle down to be civil agin, it was morn likely in a Yank branched plant.

Despike all that, yer post-time was lookin' good, and yer boom didden turn into a bust. Now that our Armed Enforcers was back home to have childern of their own fer a change, they found the Guvmint was eggin' them on by handin' out Baby Boners. This was one way of makin' allowance fer the famly and gittin' on with yer Copulation Explosion. Them as had no childern to speak of could apply to yer Apartment fer Veterans Affairs. (Called fer short yer Deviationists.)

✳ Yer Post Goes Boom

Not only babies was boomin', everything else seemed to be buddin' too. Out in Sasquatchewan, the new Premeer Tommy Duglass was tryna git peeple to be more sociabul about their medecine so that we cood git sick and have childern fer free. Edmunton way they was gittin' oil by lickin' the tar outta ther sands, and they got a lot more after they blew Le Duke. This sure saved the bakin' of that Sociable Credit bunch who was Ernestly Manning yer Alberter guvmint. Labbydoor struck it rich too. They was financed by Yanky oarmasters who kept ironin' out the ground and shippin' it home frum yer ex-port of Set Eels. Even yer far North was aglow now that we had enter yer Atomickle Age. Gagger Counters hard by Grate Bare lake was clickin' with Yer-ainum. Even farm peeple got in on all this effluents, and some of us ended up electryfride and flush with tilets. Canajuns got used to bein' consumptive and got more and more possessive about ther mateerials.

Wun of the reesons our boom never down-terned is we had a new enema to keep us ternin' out new weppins. Now that the Nasstys frum Hitler's Gepasto had all took refuge in Oblivia, our wore-time alleys yer Serviets seemed to fill the armymint maker's bills. Speshully after a liddle Roosian Embarrassy clerk name of Eager Goosed-stinko

spilt the beens about his fella Reds actin' up as Northern
Spys round about Ottawa's parts. Little Eager had a dickens of a time gittin' all this across in Ottawar. Most of the
peeple he tride to tell his story to ignored him. First off he
went to that noosepaper, yer *Ottawa Urinal.*
They tole him to go up the street and bother
yer Just-Is Departmint. The Secure Gard there
tole him to cum back in the mornin.*

❖ FAMOUS
FEETNOTE

Goosestinko appeared
on yer Frontal Page
Chalice with a pilla-slip
over his head, and becuz
nobuddy noo who he
wuz, he becum a true
Canajun celebrititty.

When this under-yer-covers scandle was
relaid to Primer Minster the King, he was
bizzy havin a speerchill see-ants with his ded
dog and his muther. So he tole that liddle red
clerk to take his funny papers back to the
Roosian M.B.C. But the longest Primer Minster we ever had was allways playin' both ends agin the
middle, as he never let his on-the-one-hand know what his
on-the-other-hand was doing. Jist to make sure Canda was
doin the rite thing, our King (Mickenzy) got on the fone to
that liddle Hairy Trueman who had took over frum yer ded
Roosyfelt in Warshinton. (I'm sprised King didden contack
Roosyvelt with his Weejee bored first!)

✳ Reds Under Our Beds

Hairy Trueman's guvmint started to try findin' ther own
Serviet spys, and they went lookin' fer those peeple who
wanted to overthrow the U.S. guvmint, besides Republick-
ans. But it was one of them rite-wingys, Sentaur Mick
Carthy who claim to have snuff out the most Commonests,

speshully in his Estate Departmint.* Don't
think this kinda thing didden spillover into
Canda. Wernt long before yer Amerkens was
tellin' our Mounted to look fer Reds under
our beds. They cum up with some dandys:
Furry Mowat and Pee-air Terdo, pluss six
members of yer Tronto Sympathy Orchester.
Ottawa passed a movement on the floor of
the CommonHouse to make our lokel Com-

✿ HIND
FEETNOTE

Accorn to yer old Geeks,
a Sentaur was a critter
with the front end of a
man and the back end of
a horse. Mick Carthy
quallyfride as the ladder.

monest Party illeagle – they went undyground and resur-
fiss as yer Rosedale Golf Club.

Mickenzy King finely quit his offiss in the Common
House to get more quality time at King Smear with his ded
muther and his dog. His Minster of Exterminal Affairs,
Looie Sin Lorrent cum in, starting a Grit terdition of alter-
nating Frenchfone Prime Minsters with Anglican-saxa-
phones. Louie was a biznissman, and 'tween him and old
Seedy Howe, they run Canda like it was a bizness. Corse,
Seedy had bin givin' us the bizness fer quite some time.

First thing Unkel Lou dun was let in Newfunlanders,
after they had bin talked into it by their Small Wood head,
who promised them unemploymint insurance and old-age
penshuns fer new born babies. Little Joey was born in a
outpost of an outport called Gambo where his famly had
live fer two hundred yeer. But Joey felt there
was somethin' fishy about where he lived,*
and he was determin to make it big in the big
sitty. When he dun that, by becumming a
urbane noosepaperman, raddio star and pig
farmer, he thought every outporter should do
the same, wether they liked it or not.
(Nowadaze they'd call him the Rambo of

✿ FISHY
FEETNOTE

He wuz mebby rite
about them fish, witch
started to disapeer
when trawlin terned
into a big drag.

Gambo.) Turns out they didn't much, and when he held a
plebskite fer to enter Canda, menny thot it was too close to

Joey dun it all

❖ REDALERT
FEETNOTE

Yer Due Line was a erly nukuler detergent. It stood on gard fer thee and me and yer hole of yer Ewe Ass way up there in them high Articks. Only time that line got reely buzzed was the day Northamerker was put on a lurt on account of a flocka geese. Thank God sumbuddy on yer raidar was a naycher luvver and pervented them stuporsonic bummers frum bein' goosed into ackshun.

❖ OLD TESTY
FEETNOTE

That'd be yer Oh Nan, who seem to have invent yer laying on of hands.

call, but he drug all of them kickin' and screemin' into Canda ennyways.

Looie also wanted to bild the Sin Lorrent See-way to take away bizness frum Sinjohns and Hellfax, but he cooden manage to float aloan so he settle fer a Transcanda Hiway and yer Dueline.✶ Like Sir Johnny Macdonald, Uncle Looie Sin Lorrent had a dream of a nashnul stream of cars goin' acrost Canda without ever havin' to dip into yer States. But them low Yank gas prices have druv menny a Canajun below yer 49 parlells of lassitude. That hiway out west maid sure that ninety pursent of Canajuns now live within a hunderd miles of the border, so the Trans Canda Hyway seems to of bin maid fer crossborder shop-in.

Canda made a good livin in them days, sellin' off our nacheral race-orses and bankrollin' Yankee branched plants, but cum 1950, five years after our end of hostillitities, times wasn't all that good enny more. We had boomed fer haff a decadent, then the hole rig started to sputter, coff and spit out chaff. Some say it was yer U.S. Martial Plan with their Forinade Dispenser that dun it. They was subsistin' ther own farmers so's they could ship wheat to Auntie-Commonests in Yerp fer to keep ther Goodwill. That left us Canajun grain-groars holdin' our full bags. We had weet comin' outta our ellyvators untill we was spillin' our seed on the ground like that fella in the Bible.✶

Funny enuff in them sirpluss yeers, the one good cus-
tomer we had was yer Serviet Onion, mainly on accounta
yer Yank had open up a Cold Wore with them, and us Canajuns wasn't quite so fridge-id. Too bad we dint reckanize a
billyun Chinee when they kick out yer Shank-High Chex
and brung in yer Masty Tung. We cooda empteed the barly
outta our bins, but we sheepishly strung along with yer
Yank.

✳ Yer Kareer Wore

Since yer Un-nightied Nations had bin in the bizness of
wirld guvmint, peece seem to be reerin its ugly hed pritty
regler. Then alluva sudden, the two Kareers, Norse and
Souse, started snarlin' on their backfence, and ended by
mixin' it up on the border in their 38 Parlell Bars. I fergit
witch evaded the tuther, probly yer Norse jumped on yer
Souse, but before yuh could say Jackie Robinson, liddle
Hairy Trueman brung in his Nummer One Genrul, Big
Dugs MacArfer. Canajun troops, always lookin' fer a liddle
action, went along fer the ride. Some of them got to be
prizners too, but thanks to yer Red Crossers they got ther
parcels every munth. Their hosts maid sure they got their
brains warshed every Sardy nite.

Hairy Trueman was afrayed that the Roosians was
stayin' outta this conflick jist so's they could evade Yerp
wile everybuddy elts was in the Kareering Capitall pre-
occupying Sole. Biggern that was the fack that them Red-
niks had stole our copyrites and bilt their own atomical
bums. Both sides was now bizzy into Preparation H bums,

makin' big jets fer to carry them radium-active missals, and threttening to drop ther lode on eech uthers. That's how cum the Yanks start up yer Norse Atlantical Entreety Orgynization fer to keep everybody on their NATOES. Canda went along, cuz they needed some occipational therpy fer their millinery peeple to do after Kareer.

So what was the upshat of that Kareer ruckus? Nuthin' change fer yer Kareerans. They bin hagglin' over yer 38 parrlell bars ever sints. Fer the rest of us, it was the same as before after every war. Tern yer sords into plow shares and line up fer yer pogey. Peeple git vurry neuralgic when they look back over ther sholders to ther pastyeers. War seems to be the best times that most of them remembers ever having, and you'd be sprized at how menny is jist dyin' to git into anuther one.

✳ Arts and Culcher: A Messey Report

Vinny Messey, Queen's Repry-hensitiv

Some say Canda finely cum of age when they got ther own home-groan Guvner-Genral. First lokel boy to move into Redo Hall was Vince Messey, hair to yer Messey-Harse thrasher-binder forchune, witch for Varity later committed merger with sumbuddy elts and becum Messey-Fergoosin. Fer some one reered on farm implimints and aggravaculcher, Vince Messey had more the look of a town-boy, took to them claw-hammer coats and cutaway pants as to yer manor borne. Talked like he was raised up in a house of lords, too. Mebby that's cuz his last job afore this had bin over to London, Angland, where he was livin' High on Commission.

The thing that clinch his anointment as the Queen's repryhensitiv in Ottawa was probly that Messey Report he got off on Canajun culcher. Up till that time the only culcher round our parts had been eether agri or horti, with the odd shot of pencilinen. But with all the effluence around yer post-wore peeriod, Canajuns started takin' ther baby bonusses and payin' a baby-setter so's they cood step out a bit. Some found their vocations by takin' two weeks off in the summer. They sure found their way round our parts in Muskokey and a lotta them romped and plaid with therselfs while the wife and I was swettin' tryna git in the hay.

But vocations got nuthin' to do with culcher accorn to Valeda. Culcher fer her is lissening to classified music plaid by a sympathy orchester – that stuff that keeps threttnin' to tern into a toon and sumhow never duz. If the wife don't git a good dose of that stuff every cuppla weeks she gits as rangy as a cut cat. That's why she goze regler to that Festervill of yer Sound up our way every summer along about gang-thrashin time.

Yer Messey Report didn't stick to yer amusements – it got morn a few backs up when it cricketsized Canajun Universallys by sayin' they was too provinshul. I never heerd of a Federast school fer hire lernin, but Vince wasn't talkin' bout nashnulizin' colleges. He jist wanted our uppity eddication schools to be as good as the ones in England when he waltzed thru Camebritches in his Oxfords.

Shakespeer-on-Tario

But it was yer Shakesbeer that put the cap on all this. When the dotter of George yer

Sexth got coryonated in West Minister's Abie, Tom yer Pat-
ter's Son was a-festerin' to bring the Beard of Avon to the
banks of Stratford-On-Tario. But them banks wasn't
intrusted in puttin' ther money in sich a artsy-fairy idee, so
Tom got some lokels to becum a Bored, and they all shell
out fer the airy-fare to bring out Toney Guffey, the biggest
Shakespeering fella in Angland (he was sex foot sex) fer to
tell them Stratfurters how todo much without nothing.

That was farty yeer ago but their Festerall rig is still
havin' its runs every summer. There's a blanched plant of
this outfit hard by Nagger Falls witch is give over to the
skits writ by a Saint Bernard, Pshaw.*

But with all this uplift there was a new
meejum on yer hore-izon. It was call Tella-
vision, and it was the wurst thrett to culcher
since bubblegum. Fer insted of goin out to fes-
teralls and consorts, peeple begun to be
home-bound, eatin' their dinners offa frozen tin-trays with
ther eyes fix on Meltonburl, Loosey Balls and Howdy Doo-
doo.

I dunno what Vince maid outta Canajun TV, witch start
up about fore yeer after them Yank. Yer CBC was the only
game in town, but all this was mostly a snow-job till they
got that cow-actionabull cable. It helped too when they put
up their first saddle-lite name of All-U-wet witch was shot
up in the air fer to give us our transmissions frum coasta
coast.

All this frust-rate Vince Messey so much he resined his
job at Riddo Hall and apply fer a greencard. He figgerd if
yuh can't beet the baggers you mite as well jine 'em, and he
end up in Hollowood on that TV serious "Yung Dr. Killdeer."

✳ Immugrence Is No Excuse

Ever since Canda joined yer Untied Nations and yer Briddish Cuminyerwealth the world has beet a path to Canda's doors. After Joey Smallswood's industerearial policy fer Newfunland turned the inhibitants of its out ports into exports who went screeching down the road to the rest of Canda, Yerp started to foller. First cum yer Angled-Sacksons and yer Kelts, but soon other Yerpeens, Eyetalians and Porchgeese, cum and dropped ther bags. Hungryaryans was next after their Serviet overlards chase them out of Buddypest fer bein' too revolting.

We wernt sitch a Dumbminion of Britten any more. Insted we was becumming one fer Warshinton. After all, most of our fiscal affairs was still run by Seedy Howe, a bornYank, and his next big projeck was bildin a pipeline fer to keep Canajuns and Amerkens fulla gas. He tride to pass his gas bill thru the Common House in reckerd time by evoking what they call "close yer." This reely means close yer eyes, hold yer nose, and let my gas pass.

But this was wreckning without a big private member of the Tory Oppsit Position, John Doofenbeaker. Born of immigrunce pairents, he was noan as the Prince of Saint Albert* and was noted as a lawyer who went on the offensiv rather than jist sitting on defence.

He burst old Seedy Howe's pipeline

✿ OPPSITPOSITION FEETNOTE

Valeda sez his name was Deefenbaker, not Doofenbeeker, but then she sez I always have trubble with my vowels. And he cum frum yer Prince, not yer Saint Albert. Sho's not sure that he cood be describe as the Saint of Prince Albert.

dream with a loud pop when he give a fullabluster speech that went on, it seems, fer daze on end.

Old Seedy passed his motion all rite, but that gas left a sour smell, and spelt the end of thirty years of I dunno howminy Grits. The Tory leeder George withDrew, and Uncle Looie Sinlorrent was thinkin' of leavin' his rains to the fit-to-be-bowtied Lister "Fer the luv a Mike call me Mike" Pierson.✶ But he stuck it in fer one more go, cuz his Grits all sed they'd run him "stuffed" if necessary. But when Canajuns went to the poles, they tole a lotta them Libreeals to git "stuffed." John Doofenbeeker won a minorty vickery.

With a funny forn name, he made sure there was lots of other immigrunt monickers in his Cabnut too. To Deef a Canajun didn't need no hy-fen.✶ John Deef didn't fergit the first famlys of Canda eether: Jim Gladstone, a Blud Indyan frum Elberta, was anointed to that preevious all-White reserve, yer Senate. And Big Cheef Deef include in his cabnut the most countryversial and neeglected minorty of them all – the first feemail minster in Canda's histry, Ellen Fairglow. She wasn't give jist any portfoolio in a storm – she was maid Secetairy of the State. Canda's culcher under Deefenbaker was terning out to be a multy big thing.

✿ NO-BELL
FEETNOTE

Listerbee Piercin was a sibble serpent terned dipplemat. He got the No-Bell prize fer his effurts in the Shiny Eye Dessert after yer Sue-us Crisis.

✿ MARITAL
FEETNOTE

Valda sez most wimmen she knows wait till their weddin nite fer to give up their hyfen. Chastity begins (and ends) at home.

✳ Yer Deef in One Era

Canda had bin pritty well Grit sints the middle of yer Deep
Depression. Ackshully Deef had beat Uncle Louie by only
five seats. Unkle Looie sed good-by right after the leckshun
and handed the mantel to Peer-son.✳

Deef sniffed a big win over the new leeder Peer-son of the Oppsit Position if he called
anuther election with a quick snap. He didden wait long to do it. Fer the secund time
within a year voters got the chants to exercise ther French-fries. Tory Deef took a train
and dun a toor de farce of whistlestops
acrost Canda. Every time he stop the peeple
whistled as he pubicly addressed them frum
the back end of his scaboose. Didden hurt
that his firey glair was seen on black-on-
white tellyvision, while poor Pearson was
behind the Times, lispin' his way on the raddio. Them Libberals was completly run-
down by that Tory train. Even Cuebec give
Deef 50 of its 75 seats, tho' they probly needed sub-titles fer to understand when he spoke the Garlic
langridge. The score was 208 to 49 with 9 Western
Socialites on the side. The CCM figgered they needed a new
veehickle, so they went outta the by-cycle bizness and was
reborn as yer Nude Democrappic party.

Them socialites was doin' much better in yer pervinshul legiblature of Sascatchewin ware leeder Tommy

✣ UNDERWATER
FEETNOTE

Looie St. Lorrent
immoralized his own
name when he finly got
the St. Lorrent Seeway
bilt. It was dun with
American capitolists
and U.S. Stealers. It put
a lotta Canajun towns
under water but
brought all that Labby-
door arn ore down to
Cleeveland Ohiyuh or up
to Thundymug Bay
(witch at that time had
a dubble life as Port
Arfer and old Fart
Willyum).

Duglass brung in Meddlycare, witch maid all the doctors bring up their objeckshuns. But the Premeer put a preemyum on helth care back in them daze, jist like there is now under Roy's Romanoze.

Deef had made a shampain promise that he wood roll back yer Cold Wore, and he didden want no atomical bums on his Canajun Voodoose.*

✿ AIRY
FEETNOTE

Valeda thinks Voodoose is sumthing to do with chicken blud, but I checked yer Fax and it was a jetsetter plane we bot frum them Yanks.

At the same time Deef give the chop to our own millinery aircraff industry by shafting Canda's home-groan soupey-sonick fighter plane, yer Avro Arra. This sent about fourteen thou aircrapworkers down to yer States lookin' fer jobs, and some of them end up in yer Hewston Asterdome helping the Yanks git their rocks offa the moon.

✿ RUNNING
FEETNOTE

That'd be yer Nike that's a missal, not a joggin shoe.

The next election was fot over wether we was gonna be nukuler or nooterd during the cumming Army-geddon. Mike Pearson shoulda bin called Mike the Nike* durin' that shampain, cuz he had bin agin the idee of goin' Nukey. He musta took the oaf of Hippocrisy on the shampain trail cuz he was now all for a bit of Nukey.

By this time Deef was gittin' kinda parry-annoyed about all them Yanks in Warshinton tellin' him what to do. He didden even git along with their new sharmin yung Cheef of Stait, John F. Kennyday* when the two met at the Kennyday summer cottedge hard by Martha's Graveyard at Hy Anus Port. And when Kennyday return the Stately visit to Canda, Deef had him plant a tree so big it strained the yung prezdent's back, and put him off his feet fer more trivyal purrsuits.

✿ EFFING
FEETNOTE

I dunno wat the "F" in his name stud fer, but Valeda sez it probly defers to all his extrymartial affairs.

But it was when the Roosian leeder Khruschen started sending nukuler missals to

Fiddle Casteroil in Cuber that the ferteliza reely hit the air-conditions. Yer Yank was pritty antsy about Cuber but not neer so parry-anoid as them Cubists was about yer Yank after they got evaded at the Bay-ing of yer Pigs. When Kruschen and John F. Kenny square off it look like Hy Noon tween yer Yanky white hat and yer Serviet blackhat. Everybud-dy in the hole of yer world was hold-ing its breth eggsept possibly Deef who

Deef sits this one out

dint bleeve the thrett was all that seeriuss. Canda had bin selling train injuns to Cuber, and he was sure that them Cubists had no loco motives to cause trubble. Deef figgered the hole sheemuzzle as a bit of a a ten-test in a peepot.

Deef had hiz own innernashnul doin's, namely he got South Afferker kick out of yer Birdish Come-on-wealth, not to be let back in agin until they had got rid of ther apart-heds. Fer us farmers, he bucked the U.S. govmint and razed the hackles of their Stately Departmint by selling Canajun wheat to China.

All the time Deef was in charge he was nervous bout all them sibilant serpents that surrounded him in Ottawar.* He figgerd that they was all true-bloo dyed in the red Libberals, and he would have pee-furred to put the Eest Blocks to every last one of them. This problem has left morn one Tory Prime Minster on the horns of an enema, wondrin' if all sibble serpents are Librals, or all Librals sibble serpents?

✧ PEERIOD FEETNOTE

The wife and former sweetart thinks he was suffrin' frum yer PMS: Prime Ministeerial Sus-pishuns.

Bow-tyin' Mikc was waitin' in the wings. He had bin one of them Federast paper chasers, and knew how to swim with the red-tape tide, not agin it.

So when they went to the pollen booths the next time,

Deef becum yer ex-Cheef, and "I like Mike" was in. It didden help that the Tories had a big broo-Hees-haw of a scandle about a Jermin good-time girl, Gerty Munsingware, who had becum a secure risk by presentin' her breefs to members of Deef's Cabnut.

Deefenbaker mite not know it, but in deefeet he was goin' back to where he had allways dun best, razin' hell with the party in power frum his bench in Her Majestic's Loil OppsitPosition.

Them Grits had ther own scandles and Deef's big moemint cum when a druggy deeler, Loose'un Reevard, was aloud to excape frum jail – he was sent out to flud the prizzen skatin' rink when it wasn't cold enuff ta frosta pumkin and he used the hose to git hisself over the wall. This resulted in a wanta confidents vote in the Common House that made poor old Prime Minister Pearson cum puffin' back frum his winter vocation. Meentime that hoser Loose'un Reevard was havin' his vocation down in Floridder scotch-free.

Call me Mike for heaven's sake!

But still old Deef felt he was no longer in his glory, and would never git the chants to bring about his pet projecks: his northern dubble vision where he could see yer Articks completely inhibited with peeple in plastickal bubbles living on solo energy.

He did git his wun pet projeck into the books: he was the first to fashion fer Canda a Billy rites, witch never becum part of our Constitutional, but looked nice on the wall of yer Sibble Liberty peeple's office. He also give us our first French-Canajun Guvner-General, the well-luvved Jorge Van-yay.

Deef give us sumthin' else: never a dull moment when he was around.

✳ Quiet!! Revolution

Wun reason Deef lost that eleckshun was because he had
ignored Cuebec with his undivide attenshun. They had give
him all them seats and he just went stompin' off through
his old happy hauntin' grounds in yer West after a few
"Maize ameeze Canay Jens." Deef had never botherd to
fratternize or patternize with them Cuebec EmPees, and
his only Cuebec alloy had bin the laid Premiere Moe-Rees
Duplexes. Moe had bin the Godfather of all them Habby-
taunts, but could no longer "coopay le mootard" fer Deef on
accounta he had "kickaid le Bouquet."*

La Belly Provence was about dew to go
thru the changes after bein' run by this few-
dle dickytater who thot of all them provin-
shals as a part of his famly, like yer Cosy
Nostrils. Hooever it was that tuck over yer
Yewnion Nation-ale Party frum Duplexes
and tride to run the province in the same
Mafiasco stile didn't last too long.*

The pervinshul eleckshun that follerd
was a case of two strikes and yer out. The
Cuebec Grits didn't let the voters forgit that
Assbestus Strike, even though it had happen ten yeers
before. Them Yewnion Nationales hadden done nothin'
about the stompin' of the workers durin' that laborious dis-
puke and Cuebeckers was still bumping their gums about
it. Even the Catlick church had tern agin the Onion Nashnul guvmint on that one. That strike also brung a rich lay-
about naim Pee-air Terdo into Union pollytics.

The other Cuebeck strike everybuddy was tockin' about had bin much more reesent and it activated another Cuebecker, Reamy Leveck into gettin' pollitical. The uprising was aginst yer Raddiocanada, (Cuebeckwaz fer SeeBeeSee) and Leveck, who had bin Cuebeck's most poplar broadcastrater,* was one of the most striking strikers.

Up till that time Reamy had bin a forn cornspondent who had come home to Cuebeck tellyvision to lecher on internashnul affairs with a peesa chock and a blackbored. But durin the strike, them CBC burrocraps terned Leveck into a flame-in Nashnulist, and he offerd hisself to the Libbreal leeder Jean Le Sage (John the Wise) as a provinshul candied-date. He was a nacheral excommunicator, not pompuss like most pollytishuns, but nacheral and down to yer erth with his shrugs and his liddle smile that lasted mebby a haff a secund, and his constant butt hangin outta his mouth.

The loud part of yer Quiet Resolution reely started up after yer gangboss of yer CPR, Don Old Goredun maid a dum reemark about how he never had any French-Canajun Vice-Precedence cuz they didden have the propper Universally train-ing. Sumbuddy checked up on him and found that only seven outta thurty CPR vice-prezdents had bin to collitch, and wun of them wasn't Goredim hisself who had jist barely bin matrickulated outta hyscool. Young Frenchfones bernt him in F.A.G.* and next day they spilt paint over Queen Victorious's statute at Ma Gill Universally, and the follying week the furst bom went off in a Cuebeck male box.

French Canajuns was tired of bean treeted as thurd wirld secund class sittyzens. There was other young Cuebeckers hangin' round with a lotta new idees, and most of them was stayin' up late, (and sleepin' in late) while puttin' out a liddle maggotzeen called *City Libber*. There was Gerrard Peltyer, Jean Marshwand, Jeans Drapout, and Robber Boorasser, but the one becum best noan I spose was a weerdo intellckshul with lotsa money and a straggly beerd and roaming sandals. Fer tho' Pee-Air Illiot Terdo drest in them days like yer averidge down-and-out (what they used to call in them daze a beetlenick) he was reely a sunuva rich father frum Outraymont who had left him a lotta inhairitants to travel round the world. But he becum a socialist rather than a socialite.

When he was in Muntree-all Terdo hung round yer *City Libber* office doin' a lot of nuthin'. It allways took Pee-air a dickens of a long time fer to git his thots in print. As they say in the Garlic langridge "ou est la plume de ma dillytant?"

If he'd bin on the bredline I'll bet he wooda met his dedline. Him and Reamy Leveckyou was first-rate tockers, not riters. Whenever they met, witch was not offen, cuz Leveck was allways late and Terdo was extry punkshill, they got along like two tomcats on a back fence. Reamy figgered Pee-air fer a Federast and Pee-air consider Reamy tairbly provinshul. Leveck found in Terdo the same kinda arrowgance that he had found in Muntree-all Anglican Saxafones and in the back of his mind he determine to seprate frum sitch peeple as soon as possibull.

Oui, eh?

When they went their seprit ways, Terdo went off to the nation's capitol and becum a Libral candied-date even tho' he had uptill now acted like an End DP and cricketsized them Grits sumthing offal. Leveck was a Libberall too, and LeSage maid him Minister of yer Works, ware he reely give the peeple of Cuebec the works when he nashnalized Hydro Cuebec.

Reamy wasn't the only wun makin' yewconmick plans. 'Round the saimtime, yer Ottopack 'tween yer States and Canda got Simonized by that Reesman. If that's any eggsample of Free Trades, no wonder it got poplar with a lotta biznessmen. But ever sints yer reel Free Trades cum in a cuppla yeer ago, all our auty motives is under suspishun frum yer Yanks, who now clame we can't ship Jap knees cars acrost the border. They say they ain't maid enuff in Canda cuz Honda makes the parts grow absent.

✳ Yer Sín-Tenníel

In 1967 all Canajuns celibated what the Fathers of Conflagellation had whip therselfs up a hunderd yeers before. As part of Canda's growin' up out of its addledlessons and becumming its own boss, Lessly Piercin' decided to put up a new Canajun flag and let yer Union jack off. There was all kinds of desines, some of them wood make yiz laff fit to bust, but the winner what was choze was the plainest, simple-minded of all. When a lot of Canajuns first saw it, they thought it was the opening of a new gasstation. There was a dickens of a lot of rangling in Parlmint but we finely got it in time fer our Sintenniel berfday.

Right after our flag debait cum the biggest dust-up since World War Eleven. It started up amung our armed farces when the Nationally Defensive Minister Paul Hellyer decided to eunuckficate our soljers, sailers, and airyplane fellers. This ment that everybuddy was to share jist the one unyform.* Didden affeck yer army neer as much as our flyboys and yer navels, becuz everybuddy was give a

Valeda don't think that sounds too saniterry.

kinda green garbitch bag (one size fits all) that maid them look like they was tagging cars in frunta park-in meeters. Several admirables resined on accounta this, and they got the Hellyer outta there pritty fast.

Lookin' back a quarter of a centurion later, our Sintenniel seems to have bin Canda's finesse tower.* It was yer big Expose in Muntry-all that was the crown-in glory of our happy yeer. Called "Man and his Whirl" it was got up by their liddle French mare Jeans Drapout. It brung the world (well, at leest fifty millyun of them) to Canda's doorstop, and what they seen, they liked.

One of the big visiters was Genral Gall frum France. He sure lived up to his name when he publicly undressed a crowd frum a Muntry-all City-hall balkany, and ended up with a few words that becum a new rally cry fer the separators: "Veev yer Cuebeck Leeb!"*

Cuebec is a big milk province, basking in its dairy-air, but Genrull Gall terned out more separators that day than Alice Chalmers and John Deer coulda sold in a yeer. I think it give Reamy Leveck the push he needed fer to seprate frum the Librals and start thinking about a new idee: Sovern-titty Assassination. What that means to us Anglophonys is that Cuebec wants a divorce frum us and hopes to live offa the allymony.

This musta put the wind up the Grits in Ottawar cuz they had jist anointed a commission to bring in yer Buyculcherness and yer Buy-lingamalism. This Commission becum noan pritty soon as yer Bye-bye becuz a lotta Cuebeckers was startin to feel that way bout the rest of us in

> ✿ STOLEN FEETNOTE
>
> Valeda clames I have crabbed that frum the famous woretime speech of Winsome Churchle, and she reminds me that his finesse hour consist of nuthin' but a old rotten roll groop, Blud, Swett and Teers.

> ✿ FAST FORWARD FEETNOTE
>
> Valeda claims Pee-air Terdo dun the samething to Fiddle Castroil in Havanner a few yeer later when he hoist his glass of rummin' coke and shout out "Veev le Cuber Leeb!"

Canda. Them Cuebec-wuzzes was consern that they mite lose their own langridge and morn a few of them thot that Cuebeck should mebby be Yewnick-lingamal.

Now Terdo dint agree. He felt Cuebeckers should feel as much at home at yer Caligari Stampeed as they would durin' yer Sin John Papoose Day prade. He felt his missyun in life was to bring his fella Cuebeckers outta the back woods and into yer modren whirled.

Ottawar spent a lot of munny makin' with the bylingamal. They shoulda spent the munny fer to give them lessens to young scoolkids, insted of yer middle-ages sibbilant serpents. Keith Spicy was in charge of yer buy-lingamalism and fessed up that them perversion courses the guvmint was givin' its EmPease wasn't worth a pincha kooflap. Why didn't they start with teenyagers on their summer vocations? Send them down to Cuebec and let them fall in love, that's the best way to make time with eech other and lern to say "Quelle hoor Estelle?"

By this time Terdo had got his seat in yer Common House and it wernt long afore Lister Pearson brung him into his cabnut as the Minister frum Justiss. Pee-air drest more like a fidgitive frum Justiss. If he wernt waring a long black lether coat that made him look like he blonged to Hitler's Gepasto, he cum on like yer avridge hippy with his bear feet in his scandals and his asscot around his neck.

He druv round Ottawar hell-fer-lether in a Jagwar sporty car with a blonder two in tow, but he only went all the way once to our Expose. He sed he was too bizzy refarming our leagel sistern, and to give him his dew he sure passed a lotta motion on the floor of that house. Fer a deevout Cathlick he shocked yer bushwa-zees of yer middlin class. Most Canajuns was bound up in Holy Acrimony till deth did it to their parts, and they were deetermin to fite it out to ther bitter ends, but Pee-air change their

Divorce laws. He let peeple shake off their marge after what he called a brakedown of martial relations. Then he sed that the state could not do its bizness in the middle of yer bedroom. But Pee-air nock everybuddy back on ther heels when he aloud them homeosectionals to have free abortions.

You'd think the old gards of yer Libbreal party would be in historics, but the funny thing was that they started tockin him up as the next Grit leeder. Lister Peerson had got his flag, his hunderth berfdy party, and a good Ottopack with the States, but he coulden git hisself a majorty guvmint, so he was reddy to call hisself quits.

Pee-Air

The Tory party had alreddy got therselfs a new leeder that yeer when Deef had a dump after gittin' that Dalton Cramp in his side. The new fella was a Marmtider, Robber Stanfeeled, hair to a underware forchune, witch is mebby why he was well-noan fer keepin his trap shut.

He was a modest kind of a gink. Terdo would probly have sed that Stanfeeled had much to be modest about, but he had bin Premeer of Nosy Kosher, and probly run that province better than it has bin run before or sints. But peeple as didden know him would think he was a bit of a fuddly duddly. He didden go to disco-techs or consorts of rotten roll music, but he was a well-Red Tory and staid home in his lieberry with old books like "Bride and Bredjudice" by Jane Air.✱

Mebby that's why them Grits becum convince that they needed a wild kinda swinger as their next leeder. By this time there was morn onc Terdo maniac in that Libreeal cockus and the dizzeeze was soon to spred amung wimmen all acrost Canda frum she to she.

❖ FILLSTINE
FEETNOTE

Valeda sez I am betrayin' my litry iggerunce. It were Jain Austin writ that book, and Sharlit frum Bronty writ "Jane Air" frum withering hites.

95
❖

Part i
yí yí ✹

✳ Terdover Time

The yeer after our big Expose there was a Federast election, and alluva sudden Canda seem to be cuvvered with
Trudyomaniacs. Lucky Pee-air even cum to Parry
Sound on his shampain toor, and when he strip
down to his bikineeny bathin suit and dun a back
flip offa the dive-in bored of our Kiwi-anus swim-
min pool, all the wimmen of Muskoka went
strait to their balliett boxes and dun a flip over
him. Includin' Valeda Drain Farquharson who
sed she voted fer him becuz of his bloo eyes
and his brown belt, witch he had got frum
doin' the Judy-o. I tole her I had a brown
belt too. It held my pants up, but that didden
meen Terdo's belt could do the saim fer Canda.

Showtime!

Wun of the mane reesons Terdo was up fer Primed
Minster was cuz the resta Canda thought he was the
only fella could deel proper with Cuebeck. They felt even
moreso when Pee-air went to Muntry-all fer the Sin John
Papoose day prade. Them seprators was out in full farce,
and they kep chantin' "Terdo Oh Potto!" witch is Garlic fer
"Terdo to the Stake!" and they wasn't deferring to
Moyshee's restrunt eether. When one of their Indy-pendance
leeders, Pee-air Burgo, was ast to accumpany some

members of yer Arsy M.P., Burgo thought he was bein' excort to the revue-ing stand to sit with Terdo. Insted he was invit to sit in a patty-waggin, and when his folly-ers found that out they erupp in a fewry, throwin' coke bottles at them pollytishuns on the revue-in stand. Every one on that stand never took any stand, but tern tail and fleed – eggsept Terdo, who stud his ground wile all round him in the frackass 83 sivilly-uns and 43 pleece was took to the hosspiddle.

Poor ole Robber Stansfeeled didden have a chants. Not only was Terdo a heero on the barcades in Muntry-all, but pitchers in the paper showed Pee-air doin' the boogie-loo like he was one of them Beetlebugs frum Liverd-pool. In the saim paper wud be a fotygraft of Jist Plane Bob, the pride of Truero, Nosy Kosher eether peelin' a bananner or droppin' a football. The Torys tride to git Bob with it by havin' him git up on stage with the nudey cast of "Hair" and froog hisself a bit, but it didden catch at yer poles.

Stansfield strips fer action

When the votes was count up Terdo had morn dubble the Tory seets and Stansfeeled was thru the trapped-door and out on his undyware on the Oppsit Position benches.

First thing Terdo dun was to declare that Canda was gonna be a Just Sassiety. He spred a lotta youth hostiles acrost Canda fer yung hippys and some of them becum the Cumpny of Yung Canajuns, witch sounded like a rip-off of yer U.S. Peece Corpse. Their numbers was swole by reel Amerkens who jump acrost our borders to avoid servin' in Veet Nam, jist the same way our benighted Umpire Royulists done as the Draft Dodgers of 1776. Canda becum awarsh in yung peecenickers with napsax crossin' our land jist like them hoboes in the thirtys. Them Yung Canajuns ain't nowares to be seen now. Mebbe they terned into Amway Salesmen or are linin' up at Fud Banks. One thing fer sure, their all into their middling ages now and they'll hafta trust peeple over thurty.

Besides them pertestin' peescorpers was our big biznessmen, the Cumpny of Old Canajuns, who lined up to make three hunderd millyun dollar a yeer sellin' mewnishuns to Warshinton's War Corpse, yer Pant-leg-on. Them tyfoons is still around in a big way, tho' not nessarily in Canda. But whatever happen to yer Just Sassiety? Nowadaze it seems like Canda reely belongs Just to Sassiety peeple like Tremor Eatin and Comrad Black.

Pee-air was the idle of Anglow Canda by dent of his tuff deelins with Cuebeck, but nobuddy knew the haff of what was to come. Reamy Leveck had start up his Peek You party, but there was a bunch on the far side of his left called yer Effel-Cue. Their ideer of reeching out and gittin in touch with sumwun was puttin' bomms in male-boxes.

Then they got the idee of kidnappin' a forn dipplemat to be held as a hostidge. They picked on a Briddish fella, Gym Krotch,* cuz nuthin was more forn to them than a died-in-the-wool Anglishman. They held him fer rancid in a rotten liddle room, and writ out a Many-fisto witch they wanted red over yer Canajun Broadcorpsing Castration. But the massage

of yer Effing-Cues was totally ignore, witch prooved that nobuddy in Muntry-all lissens to yer CBC. So them terrierasts went domestic and capchured the Minister in Laber, Pee-air La Porte. (And later on, when that didden work, they fair-maid La Porte.)

Terdo called up Cuebeck Premeer Rubber Boorasser and tole him he was takin' over. He announce he was passin' the War Mezzzurer's Axe becuz they was in the middle of a appryhensive insured erection witch could end in a Cooze Dee Tat. Wunce he done that, peeple could be takin' into custardy with no warnts or warnings and kept incarstrated fer weeks. They grabbed up 497 peeple – a lotta them Reamy Leveck's PeeQuew bunch; evenshully they found out only 18 of them ever had convickshuns about anything. Just about ev'rybuddy thought this kinda treetment was just fine 'cept Robber Stansfeeled and that little Sassacatchewin' DP Tommy Duggle-ass who objeck to all this. And some Cuebeckers thought *Pee-air* was behavin' like a terrierast.

It tuck time but evenchly the purple-traitors was cot. Them bastardly plodders all got a pleece excort to Mirrorbell Airport where nobuddy would see them and was export to Cuber. After he was safe, Jim Cross sed the hole rang-dang-doo was nuthin' much more than "sex kids tryna start a revel-ution." As far as I'm consern, and I am, that revlution is still goin' strong.

 Mar Grit

McKenzy King and Arby Bennett was both bachler Prime Minsters who never got therselfs into the state of Holy Acrimony (or into a state 'bout much of ennything cum to think of it.) But Pee-air Terdo was a diner out and a dancin' devil and he hadda be the most illegible bachler in Canda when he finely fell fer Mar Grit Sinkler. He had bin the rounds with all kinds of femails but nun of them was a faytle attrackshun until her. They had a candlestine courtship fer quite a while with nobuddy cottonin' on, so everybuddy was stunt when they was tole that ther 55 yeer old Prime Minster had eelope with a 22 year old umpteenager. Speshully 'sprized was them Ottawa pressmen who had bin scooped of all this poop.

When Groom Pee-air brung this bewdy back to be his bridled-sweet at 24 SUSSEX Drive, they musta gon rite to werk, cuz she brung him forth a baby boy Chrissmus Day that yeer. Not only that, but she tern the saim trick the follering Chrismuss Day. The next Chrismuss Eve they had the sheephurds waitin' on the Common House Lawn fer her to compleat the hat trick, but she had already shelled out before Hello-Wean.

In Cuebec, Reamy Leveck tride out his Party Cuebeckwazzes in a elecksun agin Robber Boorasskic. Reamy lost big: 102 to 8 becuz Boorassick sed he could give one sweet dam. It was called yer Shames Bay Projeck and it swep away the opposition.*

While the Terdos were bein' blissfully domestick, the resta Canda was bitin' ther nails down. Us and Russia was into yer Canda's Cups fer the first time, and after that first game at yer Make Beleev Gardings it looked like a freeasco fer our side. Fellas we never herd of like Yaketyshev, Anacin and Harmthem-all was waltzin' rings around the highest pade hocky plares in the world. Team Canda even picked up a cuppla booze frum ther fans.

✿ NEW YORK, NEW YORK FEETNOTE

Boo-boo is now having problems with his Nooyork backers in prepairing the seekwell, Shames Bay Sings Again.

We was beehind two games to one with a tie to our name when our boys ship out fer yer Serviet Onion. We lost the first game in Roosia so then hadda win three straits. We wun two and that maid thc last game yer tie-broker; the hole country stopped in its tracks to watch. Them Musky-vites was leedin' us goin' into yer thurd peeriod, 5-3, but we cum alongside 'em neckineck 5-5. What happen then was a kind of mirrorcull. They didden know we had a secrete wepping, and neether did we. His name was Poll Henderson, and 22 millyun Canajuns watch him floo thru the air and truck in that puck with 34 seckins to go. Canda was unite from coast to coast fer at leest 34 secunds after that goal.

Pee-air soon hit the rode with anuther eleckshun – his slogo was "LaLonde is strong", deferring to his cheef left-tenant, Marg Lalonde.✳ Terned out it weren't as strong as Terdo thought; Robber Stanfeeld pert neer beat him at yer poles. Terdo got in by the skin of 2 of his private members. He just shrug and sed that the Uny-verse was folding up as it should. But he reelized now that fer his guvmint to serfvive he would need the help of Davey Loose and his Nude Demmycraps, who had spent the last few weeks calling Canajun biznessmen "corpulent well-faring bums." So Pee-air hadda make deels with them left wingys, and that included nashnilizing gas stations by lettin' them sit in on yer Peter-o-can.

✿ **POINTED FEETNOTE**

It wernt "Lalonde is strong" Valeda sez, but "The Land Is Strong" witch only applys round our parts at spreddin time. And it ain't Marg ... it's Mark ... yer G spot should be soft on his other end.

Since Terdo hadda go to bed with Davey Loose and them socialite peeple all day in the Common House, it maid him offal tired when he got back to his home at nite. The liddle woman waited up fer him fatefully, but he went strait to bed with a buncha breefs in brown boxes so's he could git reddy fer next day's Questing Peeriod. It soon becum a frust-rate problem, and yung Marg started climein the walls, a flour child about to go to seed.

✷ Strikes and Streeks

Yeer after Terdo got back in agin by his skin, Canda led the whirld in wun partickler airya. We had more strikes agin us than yer Muntry-all Exposers. First of all, yer ferrys on both coasts went out frum Vancoover to Ueclueless and Bordom to Cape Turpentine. Tooryists was pile-up six-a-brest at both ends of our country. By the time them ship disturbers was finished hardly ennybuddy in B.C. or P.I.E. bleeved in ferrys any more. Them Charlatans started thinking bout how they was missing yer fix linx, and it's still on their gender. Up til now it's bin yer missing link but Joe Giz has give the nod to take it to the vet and git it fixed.*

Soon after them fairys bump and grind to a halt, we went off yer rails as well. After them railers woulden cum acrost, yer bilders was out on a wildcat-in-house wock-out. Then yer mettle workers got together and decide not to give anuther sheet. And then, yer Hellfax nurses went out and the streets was full of them pertesting panhandlers. If yer plummers had pulled the plug like they thretten to, it woulda bin down the drane and farewell to No Skoasher. But that pailed in comparson with the garbidge strike in Hamilton, Ontaryario. Their mountin looked green all spring with all the Gladbags pile all up it. Undytakers was out that yeer too, and I bleeve it was after Eester before they got to bury a living sole. Awdly enuff, the anal postal strike didn't happen that yeer, on accounta they sent out the strike call by mail, and nobuddy got it in time.

✧ LINKING FEETNOTE

That britch is up in the air agin. And may end up in hot water.

Next year, striking was out and streeking was in. Even Canajuns wasn't too friggid to try it. It happen during a dull hocky game at yer Maypole Leef Gard-ins; this fella step out on the ice in his sox and that's all. Cops chased after him, he run up past yer gold, yer red, yer greens and yer gray seets, but they cornerd him hard by yer gondoler where they play the nashnul antrum and they grabbed him rite by the organ.

Pee-air called another election and took Margrit on the road with him. She was the hit of yer hustings. All them goodole boys of yer press corpse hung round her like groopys, and she was snapped and miked and quota'd every day. She tole the voters how her huz-bin wernt a cold fish, but a warm luvly shy gentile guy, and Pee-air he would hang his hed and kick dirt in fronta him with his toe jist to proove it.

Pee-air won a big major-ority in that eleckshun, and it was his yung wife that dun the trick. By the end of that toor she was even thinkin' of runnin' fer a seet herself out in Norse Vancoover but her hus-bin put his vee toe on that. Pee-air thanked her in frunt of everybuddy eleckshun nite, but the nex day he went back to the Common House, and that nite went to bed with only his parlymentry breefs witch he was to prezent to his cockus next day. Mar Grit felt like a used wife ignored with her huzbin's undivide attenshun.

Reesin Pee-air was so well-hung up on his work was cuz durin' the eleckshun Stansfeeled had tole the Canajun John Q. Pubic that they should have pricey wages controlls, jist like Nixon had tride in the States. Tricky Dick stop them after three munths when he reelized they wasn't working, and went off the Goaled Standerd instead.* This coz problems

❂ FIT TO BE TIED
FEETNOTE

The whirled had pert neer had a connipshun fit when they found out gold wasn't gonna be worth 35 dollar a ounce enny more.

with our exports and when Terdo made a fuss, Nixon tole his own cab-nut he was deeling with an Asso, but Terdo had no conneckshuns with that oil cumpny.

When Stansfeeled had suggest that prices and wages should be frigidly controlled, a lotta voters thought he was jist tryna help sell his famly's undyware. But he clamed controls would stop the rot in the high cost of keepin' up living, and we should freeze it fer 90 daze; Terdo sed as far as he was consern the thing could still stand up by itself.

A yeer later, Pee-air had change his mine. Inflayshin was gittin' to be a biggern bigger problem, and Terdo had promised to rassle it to the ground. So he went fer them controls Stanfeeled had bumped his gums about erlier. I mind it was Thanksgivering weak-end Pee-air dun it. I was eetin' a secund peece of punkin pie at the time. When Terdo cum on the TV and yelled: "Titen yer belt!" I darn neer threw up.

Them controls didden work. Never do. Yuh kin put the clamp on wagers, but prices is glow-ball, they rise of ther own accort all over the world. With his kinda controls Pee-air coulden even have rassle Daisy Lewis to the ground.

Peeter Luffheed was reely upset with Ottawa's overtaxing price-fixing altitude, cuz this was the yeer oil prices tripled amung them

Pete sitting on a fartune

sheek peeple in yer Shoddy Arabian dessert and they had us all over a barl. Bleeve it or not, the shortage was reely caused by an obskewerd Golf oil esszeckativ name Monro Bathbun who decided all by himself that Arabs was gittin' too much munny for their oil. Cooden of bin much, cuz we was only payin' two buck the barl retale. Them Arbs had a snit-fit and put an unbargo on oil, till she got up to pert neer forty dollar the barl. The upshat of this dust-up was that all them computers tride to git into a carpool, and sitty peeples became streetwalkers.

To distract us frum all the price fixin' and price risin' Terdo dun sumthin' sneeky. Since he coulden give us cut-rate prices he give us cut-rate tempachures insted. Without tellin' nobuddy, he put Canda on the Metrical sistern, mezzuring everything in cent-a-peeds. I spose that was to try and keep up with the Post Office. Ottowah tride to git us farmers to mezzure our akers in hecktairs, but we told them to git the hecktairs outta there, so the guvmint still has us all by the akers.

But all these kerfuffles was nothin' compair to the trubbles Pee-air was havin' at home. He hadda do dipers fer three liddle boys, on accounta his yuthfull shatlain had took off fer the brite lites to make moovys. I never seen any of them pitchers even on the Laid-Laid Show. Valeda thinks that the producers kep the moovys and releesed her insted. Nobuddy had a ninkling of the trubble up yer Sus-Sex Drive till Mar Grit went stag to a Messy Hall consort of the Galling Stones on her wedding analversry. She beehave like a stag at Bay while Pee-Air was at the same time lechering at yer Universally of Tronto and reseeving a honorairium degree. He told them stoogents if they coulden git a job to hit out fer the States: only person tuck his advice was his wife. She went off to a trade skool in Noo York called yer Studious 69. It was a Disky Tech fer to lern fornograffy.* After that, she writ a cuppla books about the deekline of their marge witch tern out to be best smellers.

✿ DANCIN'
FEETNOTE

Valeda sez that Studious number was only 54, and it wernt fornograffy she was lernin' to flash with, it was foetoggerfy.

Sooner than later Pee-air and Mar Grit agreed to becum Canda's best noan separators.

✺ Statues of Wimmen

Round this time yer report of yer Royal Commisshun lookin' for yer Statues of Wimmen was heard. Trubble was there weren't none to be found then and there aren't none now.* The only ones I see on yer Common House lawn is still all mail. The newest one is John Doofenbeeker and the look on his face as he smirks at the Common House tells yuh his hole story. Yer Wimmin's Rib is still waitin' fer Eekwality, even tho' Valeda thinks it would be a offal step down fer all her sects. While wimmen in yer Thurd Wirld like Injura Gandy and Goldy My Ear was runnin' countrys, we was gittin' topless shoeshine parlers so men could look down on wimmen at their work.

✿ VALEDA
FEETNOTE

There is so. One of Queen Victorious and a new sequestrian statchel of our Queen, a triboot to the only member of yer Roiled Famly likely to stay married.

Even after Intynashunal Wimmen's Yeer, Tronto's only jestyer was to erect up yer CN Excommunication towers, the world's tallest unsupported stricture in a vane attemp to teach the men of Tronto humility. Ottawar's contrybution was to put out some buttons that sed "Why Not?" Valeda wore it until young fellers accosterd her by the malls, learing at her and sayin' "It's OK by me, yer place er mine?" Valeda thinks the buttons shoulda sed "Why Not Knot?" and put the anus on men to have a vasextummy fer berth controll.

✸ Joke Lark

By the time Pee-air and MarGrit had separated, Robber Stansfeeld and yer Tories had also come asunder. Joe Clark, also noan as Joe Cluck, Joe Clutz and Joe Who?Who? had bin nummnated head of yer Tory party. How'd he get there? He was everybuddy's secund choice. First choice seem to have bin everybuddy elts, incloodin' that Clod Wagnair, "liddle" Jack Horner, Florid Mickdonald, Pall Hellyer*, Sink Steevins, and a yung snip with a voice like a bumble bee in a jug, Brine Bullroney.

Pall "Temprytoree" Hellyer was a ad-Libral who turned with the wind like the old cock on toppa my barn.

Clod Wagnair had cum up Noomyroe Yoo-noe on the first balliett. Briney was secund, and ex-static. But then the press found out that Brine and Clod had dun a durty deel in the backrooms to fit Clod with a hidden Truss. It made them reporters suspishus about all the munny that Brine'd bin throwin' about durin' the champain. The climb-it started to change, and a shnook cum up that blew Brine no good.

Joe was the dark-haired horse that cum up thru the middel and backed his way into the leed, witch was a darn gud thing fer him, cuz otherwise he woulda had to go out into yer cold crool world and get a reel job. By the thurd balliett, when that Stinker Steevins went Clarkside, Bull-roney was out in the cold on his affluence. Forth ballit, Clod Vagnair ast Briney to cum over on his side and be a Kingmaker, but Briney sed he only wanted to be a King. So it was Little Joe got the Bananza.

Joe had bin hangin round Tory party backrooms since he was old enuff to shave. He was a reel Party animal, but eggsept fer drinkin' a lotta Cokes yuh couden exackly call him a high-liver frum High River. Joe had married abuv hisself with a Mactier girl who had a mind of her own and spoke it offen. She had ambishuns to grab her own seet in Parlmint sumday. Marine was a smart bilingamal girl (oops! woman) who was becumming a lawyer, but she didden like to be called Moe Clark so she kepp her maid-in name of Mactier. This upset some old showvinist boars but delited yer faminast sows. She never call herself Mrs. or Miss but Mizz, witch sounded a bit like a wasp in heat, witch Moe clamed she was neether.*

Clooless Joe?

Furst thing Joe dun when he was elected was take Moe on a whirled-wind toor of forn parts. Along went most of yer press-gang too. This was sposed to be a kind of hunnymoon innerduction to the new Tory leeder fer the fokes back home. It was the first time most Canajuns had got a look at the yung Hed Regressive-Preservative outside of yer Common House. He allways sounded okay there, not high or wide, but sertinly Hansard. But when he went out-dores in yer Midleast, peeple watchin' ther Nashnul Snooze started to notice he was doin' a funny wock like they dun on that Mount-a-Python TV show. And when he spoke to them TV cameras it still sounded like Hansard insted of like a yuman bean.

✧ FEMAIL FEETNOTE

Valeda sez WASP stands fer White Anti-Sexual Protestant, and Moereen was a practising Catlick.

Ackshully, fer a unfit man, Joe had a heckuva lotta stamminer, and he mite of cum thru this toor intack if he hadden lost his luggridge at allmost every stop. This had nuthin' to do with him, but he sure got the blaim fer it. The press ganged up on him fer all this, but Joe never lost his tamper with them. Fer a unco-ordulated fella he sure manetaned a lotta grace under press-yer.

❋ Yer Pee-air and Reamy Show

Altho' he was besetted with martial trubbles, Pee-air Terdo never give up his day-job. He was still determin to make Canda a place ware Frenchys and Anglows cud feel at home anywares they went, even if he hisself reely didn't have one to go back to eech nite. In fack, a lotta Libreeals felt the same way in the resta Canda, becuz the only province that didden have a Tory guvmint was the liddle island of P.I.E. and the Grits kept losin' every bylerection that cum along.

Pee-air's old enema Reamy Leveck had became P.D.Q. Premiere of Cuebeck. Robber Boorasser had started the Garlicization of langridge with Bill 222 which frossted all yer Cuebeck Anglefones and give them a headake. Reamy went Booboo one better and passed Bill One Oh! One. The rapercussions reely started when that big insurience cumpny Sunlife mooved outta Muntry-all and headed along Highway Fore Oh! One to Tronto. Ottawar had maid French and English our two offishul langridges, but them P.Q.'s was content to be eunuch-lingual.

After them Separators got in power, the order musta cum down from above (not God... Terdo) to recruit Cuebeckers for under-the-cuvvers work agin the party-in-power in their own province. They was encouraged to steel papers and infilthitrate the P.Q. orgy-nization, and do a barn-burnin' job of ruinin' their party. Talk about bein' on guard for thee and me, it was yer R.C.'s M.P.'s, them mewsical riders, who broke more laws than they ever pertected. They opened peeple's males – even afore yer Watery Gates – burglarizin' P.Q.'s members hit lists at their party hindquarters. They reely did burn down a barn too, when they didden have the texnickle no-how to wiretap the rustical place where them Separators was gonna have candlestine meetings.*

The Federast government decided that the scandal should be investigorated and ordered up yer Macdonald-Feable Commission to find out what our boys in the cherry red coats and boy scout hats was up to. Sprize, sprize, they found out that mosta the public approved of our Mounties breaking the law.

Valeda sez we have a separator in our barn has never give us any trubble atall.

Wun fack that didden cum out with the commishun, but has only jist bin revealed is that Clod Moron, one of yer Hed Cabnut Separators under Reamy Leveck was doin' double deels with yer R.C.M.P.s. It don't sound like he was co-arsed into this, eggsept by the power of munny. Clod Moron was the fella thunk up the questyun fer that referee-endum that defeated Seppertizm, and even maid Reamy Leveckyou change his mind about purrsuing it. Sounds like he was reely workin' fer yer R.C.'s M.P.'s which mebby stands now fer Roaming Cathlick Members of Parlmint.

It sure was a pairaducks that the same peeple who had voted Reamy in provinshully was the ones always voted fer Terdo fedderasticly. Same thing happen later in Ontaryio. As soon as the Grits was out of offiss in the Common House, wernt long before them Queens Porker Torys seemed to git terf out.

Them Fedderastic Grits seen the writin' on the wall fer them on accounta yer Gallupin' poles. The party-in-powers had bin delayin' goin' to the poles as long as they could, but now the dye hadda be cast and Canajuns got to axersize their french-fries jist afore April Foolsday.

Terdo spent most of his shampain tocking about re-doin' yer Birdish Norse Amerka Act, and bringing our con-situtional home frum Grate Britten. That way we could stop havin' to go to them Statues at Westminster fer pre-mission to change our leagle sistern.

The three Stooges

This hole issyuh of our consit-tutional terned out to be a reel snore amung the voters. Joe Clark on the other hand was steeling some of Terdo's Gumslinger stances, and it sure help when he hook his hands in his pockets insted of waving them about like a wounded hooping crain. He still maid lotsa mistaiks tho' and when he went on TV against Pee-air and Ed's Broadbent he was so nervuss he laffed like one of them crains in heet. Eds Broadsbent tern out to be yer mas-ter-debater that nite, but when peeple went to yer poles and the ballyets was count up it was Joe Who wun the goaled, Terdo the sliver, and Broadsbent got bronzed.

✳ Yeer of a Child

JokeLark becum the youngest Prime Minster of Canda the nite before he terned farty. He was under the aprryhension that mosta the country had voted fer him, when reely what they had dun was to vote agin the fella they now called

Pee-air Idiot Terdo. They wanted Terdo out, and didden care too much at the time Who was in. Joe was only a seven-munth inhibitant of yer PEE-Em-Oh's office, witch makes his rain preemachure at best. His mane trubble was that he felt he should keep all his eleckshun promisses. I dunno ware he woulda got sitch a idee frum – sertinly not frum any other politishun. Two of them promisses was what you mite call rash – at leest they give a rash to most Torys when they finely got in offiss after all them yeers in the Opposition dessert.

First day in his offiss, Joe brung up the madder of our Canajun Embarrassy in Tel Aviz. Joe wanted it mooved to a more capital place, like Jerussi-lam, so's we wood be in the saim low-cal as other well-noan embarsees like Oblivia, Chilly, Clumbya, Costa Reeky, Equaldoor, El Saliva Door, Watta Malla, Hatey, Venusazalea and Yeraguy. Major countrys like yer Ewe Ass and mosta the resta yer Ewe Enn avoid the issyuh on accounta there was a energy shortedge on, and they didden wanna mess with them Arbs and their quotas and pintas of oil. Bellcanda and Wastinghouse and even Cana-dare was all in deep with them Shoddy Arabians too. They had a lotta Canajun employees out there in yer dessert workin fer yer sheek peeple, and they was pritty worried about Muslin retalia-nation. Suddenly Canda, the so-call peeskeepers of yer Go-lam Hites and yer Gazzy Strippers, didn't seem so nooter enny more.

Floradora Mickdonald, hoom Joe had anointed as his Mistress of Forners Affairs was beside herself (not her faverit position). She didden wanna go to yer Untidy Na-tions and have all them Arbs spit on her. She tole Joe to at least post-poan his ackshun until after Jimmy Carter had broke Camp David with an agreemint 'tween Menockim Bagels and Amoor Sedate.

✿ WET
FEETNOTE

Stanfeeled was from
Novy Kosher which is
jist this side of yer Fur
Eest in Newfyland. New
Brunsick is more yer
Middle Eest.

Even Bob Stanfeeled, Joe's Midleast ex-perk,* told Joe that makin' that move of mebby sexty mile would put all us Canajuns behind the Pail fer yeers to cum, with no oil in our bucket. It was Joe's first free-assco, but not his last.

While up on the stump he'd also promissed to privatize yer Pet-roe-can so that Canda could becum self-defishunt in oil. This guvmint oily cumpny had bin orgy-nize mostly by yer End D.P.'s when they was in bed with Pee-air Terdo back when he had run short of seets in the Common House. It becum pritty unpoplar with yer West; they called the peeple who worked in that Peetero-can bilding out to Caligari "Red Squares." They felt that the state had no bizness in the bedrock of that part of the nation.

But now it was ate yeer later and the plitickal clime-it had gone thru the changes. Yer Shaw had bin kick out of Eyeran by that old Shee-ite, Eye-tole-yuh Cockamamie, and the oil bizness was in term-oil. Them OPECKERS was puttin' the cartel before the camel and tripplin' their prices. Acrost the 49 parrlells of lassitude there was long line-ups at gasstations and a possumbility that some Cana-juns in their homes mite not be in heet all winter. Even yer private oily sextors now felt that the wun thing that gar-nteed supplys was this guvmint-run oil-can. Besides, the dam thing was showing prophets. Even the Minster of Energy, that affabull Ukey-ranian, Ray H. Natishun, alluva sudden announce that there wood be no split-up of yer Peter Can.

Jokelark was annoid, and his cabnut was more split than accord of kindlin'. Jon Crosby, the goofy Newfy in charge of all our Fiscal Affairs was makin' jokes about how eleckshun promisses didden mean a pinch of moose-shat.

Bumpy stickys was seen on cars: "Save Petro Canda, Sell Joe Clark." Joe's Cape Brettin boy, Lole Murry, now a Sentaur, and that Trezzury Boarder plutocrap Stinkler Steevens was about the only Tory haunchos in faver of degnashnalizing. Joe hisself still felt addamint bout keepin' that partickler promiss, becuz he had bin accuse of wocking around in flip-flops sints he started his ray-jeem.

The upshat of this hole rang-dang-doo was a revize virgin of yer Petrifican contrack that made it a private cumpny but with the federast guvmint as its biggest invester! More rover, every adulterated Canajun was give five free shares to boot around as they seen fit. Kids who was alive on the dait of that share issyuh hadda wait till they was ate-teen to git theirs. I dunno where yer privates enteryerprizers was sposed to fit in. This derangemint manage to infuriate Torys Eest and West, both Billy Davis in Ontaryo and Elberta's Peeter Lawheed.

The wun good thing that happen to Joe during this freeasco was that Pee-air Terdo resined hisself to bein' a private sittyzen. This let the Torys breethe eezier cuz they knew them Grits would be all tide up in a leedership prevenshun fer the next sex munths. So "Bingo" Crosby was all smiles when he put on a pare of mucklucks and preepaired to deeliver his first "boojit." It was sub-title "Short time panes fer longtime Suregains." He thought he could count on Canajuns axscepting an exercise tax of 18 cents per leeder of gass to start to pay off our nashnul defickit.

Bingo! Crosby

That dink Crosby found out later he coulden even count the arses in the seets of yer Oppsit Position benches as compair to the bums on his side. Flory Mickdonald was away in Brussles on her NATOES, and sex other Torys was away fer some persnal reesin or other. The Squeaker of the House, Jim Jrome, was a Grit anointed fer the job by Joe hisself, but if it cum to a tye he had the decide-in vote, and gess witch way he'd jump. The Grits brought in all their members fer the vote, one of them even in his hosspiddle bed who hadda to be lift up to say his nays. The Torys counted on that rite wing minorty bunch, the Sociable Crediters to vote on their side, but they jist sat in their seats and abstained them selfs.

Not-so-sheek Joe

When the role was called up yonder, the Torys was found wanton by sex, the number of their absinteasers. Joe Clark rose up in his seet and sed nex morning he was gonna visit the Guverning Genrull up yer Redo Hall. That ment only wun thing ... a Fedral eleckshun. Joe musta had vissyuns in his hed of old John Deefenbunker, who tern his minorty guvmint inside of a yeer into the biggest majorty guvmint in histry.

Joe reely haddent gotten warmed up in the Prime Minster's seet before he hadda vacate, so he hadden got a hole lot dun. His fella Torys was fewrious that Joe hadn't got around to makin' all them patteronedge appointmints of jedges and sennators and ambarsadoors before his guvmint fell in that Deesember freeasco. Joe jist sed: "I was savin' them fur Chrissmuss presents!"

✸ Yer Secund Cumming

Everybuddy agreed Joe Clark was a nice kid, kinda nigh-eve mebby, but downrite deesint when yuh got to his bottom lines. Wun nice thing he dun was not to move Pee-air Terdo out of his Prime Minsteerial office in yer Centerd Block. Joe let him keep it, which give Pee-air a peed-a-tair in Ottawar.* Three weeks before the wanta confidents vote that brung down yer Torys he had offishully took his last hooray in the Common House, follered by all his innemys prazing him to the skys.

❖ MOVING FEETNOTE

Terdo had never cared much fer Stormaway and had jist bought a Artsy Dick-o rezzadents in Montree-all fer to house "My Three Suns."

The day after the nex eleckshun was announce, Joe Clark was off and runnin' fer to git back in agin. Terdo on the other hand was preepairing to clean out his drawers and move out of his old offiss on to a more sivvil life. But his privates sexretairy, Jimmy Cahoots, had other idears. Jimmy always kept his ears close to the groundswell, partly on accounta he was bilt short, but he had a inklin that the Grits was rising up yer popillarity poles. Ever sints Pee-air had resine hisself three weeks before, all kinds of hares-a-parents had bin cummin outta the woodwerks after his job. The biggest of them was Big Donald Macdonald, no relayshin to the hamburger clown, who was all set to take over, and got shock out of his pants when Jim Cutes talked Pee-Air Terdo into runnin' agin fer Prime Minster.

Old Brainmaker Keef Davey cum in his pin-strikes suit frum the back room to orgynize Pee-air's cam-pain. Joe

Clark was allreddy on the road, gumslingin' away, and makin' jokes about poor old re-tred Terdo, who used to make even better jokes about Joe. But Davey and Cahoots had a differnt stragedy fer Terdo this time. It was called low-britching: they dusted him off but they didden wind him up.

Cap'n Terdo
on the low
bridge

The more Joe talked and squawked and funny-walked his way acrost Canda, the more Terdo's handlers maid him behave like yer Unvisitable Man. Even the pressed-gang coulden git near fer to scrum him. Jimmy Coots was the front man and it seemed as if there was no one behind him.

Nobuddy can much remember what the Unvisitable candied-date tocked about. There was no talk this time about bringin' back our constitutooshunal, even tho' we found out lader that it was on Pee-air's mind all the time. It look more like yer Grits and yer Torys had traded speeches frum last time. Here was the present encumbrance Joe tryna x-plain away all his misstaiks, and there was Terdo voiding nashnul unity. Funny thing was, at the end of the shampain trail, it was Joe who was startin' to hide frum the pressboys, and Terdo who started openin' up. Joe's jokes about Pee-air's peeky-boo stile didden go over too good in Cuebec. Terdo cum on all modest, and et in the caffy-teeria with the resta yer proletary-rats. You'd think he was doin' a rich little impressyun of Robber Stanfeeled.

The wun differents 'tween Joe and Terdo was the way they seen the fewcher of this country. Joe thought of Canda as a "cow-mew-nitty of cow-mew-nittys," while Pee-air seen Canda as more than jist the some of its public and private parts. And even if them parts rubbed up agin eech other with frickshun, Canajuns could still be intrusted in the hole. Pee-air thought Joe's plan fer the country would tern it into a confedupration of shoppin' senters.

Neether candied-date went down too good out west. Clark was still upholdin' that 18 sent gasstacks, and had alreddy commit hisself to cuttin' down on the defickit with it, and that's where he made his fokes pass.*

Terdo was makin' promises like dubble-trackin' yer CPR frum Mare to Mare and that give Pee-air a crud-ability problem. Western-ers started mummbling about becoming sep-arators like Reamy Leveck's Partly Cuebeck-wazzes. The resta the time Terdo was talkin' outta both sides of his mouth and gittin'

away with it. Peeple would say: "Do you wanta increase or deecrease our deficki?" And Pee-air would say, "I doan wanna be dog-ma-tick about it." So Pee-air cum back frum this toor an old dog with no new tricks.

The upshat of all this was that Terdo only got 2 out of 75 seets out West, but he got 74 outta 75 seets in Cuebec. So Tory Ontairy-airy-o was the wun to make up the differ-nts, and Billy Davis, the Brampton Budda-ball, was the Kink maker. He had backed Joe the time before, but tern agin him this time becuz of his gas attax.

"Wellcum to the 80's!" sed Terdo at his vickery celiba-tion. If he'd noan what them 80's was gonna be like, he mite-na bin so blaim cheerful.

✹ Yer Seperendum

The reeson Reamy Leveck had called his Cuebeckers to vote on whether they wanted to be part of Canda, "wee oo non," was becuz he figgerd Pee-air Terdo would be by that time a retard, outta-the-way seeniory sitizen. But there he was everybuddy's PET* back in ackshun and holdin' a blank check fer to reepatriot his constitooshunal.

✿ INISHUL FEETNOTE

Them three letters stand fer his three names, but Valeda sez in Cuebeck it stands fer nothin' but an old fart.

When Leveck finely pop the REFEREE-ENDUM questyun everybuddy on both sides thought it sounded kinda vaig. Terdo called it a frod. It was so fulla ware-asses and knotswithstandins that it sounded like Reamy had drawed up a will. He never ever tocked that way in pubelick, but more like them beer-drinkers in the tavs after a hocky game, F-wurds and all. It was that Peek-You intelleckshul mole, Cloud More-on, who had got to work on this simple madder, To Wee or Not to Wee, and terned it into a complycated question.

It look at first like Reamy and his Wee-side was gonna win fer sure. The No-no campain started out like a buncha alleycats all in heet on a back fents; they were fightin' with their own teem stead o' the other wun. The first face-off was a big debait in yer Cuebec City House of Dissembly. The Separators had bin primed fer this fer munths and was well-rehersed fer their Farethee Well. The Libreeals, with Clod Rine leedin' them, sounded like they'd only herd about the thing yesterday. Reamy wipe the floor with Clod and prooved he was the Masterdebater.

The Galluping Poles showed some different sadistics. It was a tie after that furst peeriod, but them Yesssers was slitely behind the No-ers by the skim off their milk (2%).

Yer Peek-you team had a tellyvision tockshow "hostess with the mostess" called Lease-a Chevette.* She got herself in trubble by calling Clod Rine's wifey Allwet.* Rine suddenly had fifteen thou more supporters – all of them Why-Vettes who made more than a quorum in yer Muntry-all Forum. But it was neer the end of the secund period and Rine needed more than help frum the bleechers.

Fer the cup playoff Pee-air "Slapshat" Terdo was called in fer to take a penalty shot. He maid 4 speeches in 4 weeks and every one of them a barn-burner. He compaired Reamy Leveck with the total-tittletarian leeders of Cuber, Hatey and Jimbobsaway. Leveck got so mad at this, in his nex speach he maid fun of Terdo's middel name (Iliot), cuz his muther wasn't French. Terdo called Reamy the raciest state-hed in Canda, and pointed out that a lotta Leveck's Peek-youse cabnut minsters had "forn" names like Pee-air Mark Johnston, Louie O'Neill and even Robert Burns!

Jeens Cretin dun his bit too – he tocked down-to-earth yewconomics like gas prices and jobs. He sed the only thing all them big Separators wanted was to becum embars-a-doors to forn countrys so's they could drive a Cattle-ack with their own fag on the hood.*

Referee-endum Day, May 22, was yer Moemont Criteek, and the voter ternout was morn 85%. I happen to be takin' a loada hawgs to Baconsfield and the wife and I stayed ware we had relations in a sluburb of

✿ SHOWBIZ FEETNOTE

Valeda sez her name's Pay-off not Chevette.

✿ SECOND FEETNOTE

Valeda sez she sed no sich thing. She called the woman a Eevette witch is the same in Anglish as calling her Mrs. Leevit-to-yer-Beever Cleever.

✿ CORRECTIVE FEETNOTE

I meant flag, not fag. I sumtimes have trubble with my continence as well as my vowels.

Montry-all. That nite I was invite to yer Pall Slovay Urena to watch the big show-down – the prize bein' the brake-up of Canda. I was surroundead by young Separators all fulla hope and glory and wavin' them Flour-de-Lease bannors. They kep waitin' fer their captain Reamy to appear. It tuck a long time, and when he did, they give him a stand-in ovulation musta gone on fer sex minits.

When the applaws dyed down Leveck hadda tell his athaletic young supporters that they had lost the game: Eyes=40 Nose=60. Not even most of the Frenchfones had voted fer Sepration. Reamy hadda say: "Wait till nex time." He dun it like a champean.

Across town, Clod Rine was celibating vickery by having a nockdown dragout argymint with Jeens Cretin. They was pert neer rasslin fer the mike-reeo-fone rite there on the Teevy. Clod took posessyun and give a twenty five minit harang that maid him sound like a sore winner.

After whiny Clod cum classy Terdo, who prazed Leveck and all his Sovern-titty Assoasyates fer keeping fathe with demockercy. The resta Canda went to a peecefull sleep that nite figgering Cuebeck was in the bag furever, and they could fergit about the hole Nashnul Unittitty nunsense.

✸ Takin' Our Constitooshunal

While Terdo was takin' on them Separators, he set out to unite the resta the country by makin' sure everyone was mad at him. He brung in Yer Nashnul Elegy Polissy jist when yer Sheek of Calgaree, Peter Lawheed, thought that his SINCrude efforts could make some money outta them oil Tarzands – as long as they got the Grits out first. But the Grits staid, and this morn anything got them Westerners cheezied off enough to start thinkin' about sepertism. Them Grits were pursonner-nun-gratin out west. At the same time, the Alberta Oppsit Position, yer Sociable Credits was ded as a Dinashores doodoo. What carried the next eleckshun was Lawheed's Torys. He thunk up Elberta's Hertage fund, which was, like its name, garnteed to pervent Elbertains from gettin' hert. It was sposed to be earning a quarter of a million dollar per deum jist by keepin' up yer interest.✶

The mornin' after yer Seperendum Pee-air had plans fer a stroll over to Number 10 Drowning Street to test the waters on that madder deer to his heart – bringin' home our BEE-END-EH? Act.

✿ FLAT
FEETNOTE

Haven't herd too much about it lately. Has Getty got at it while the Gettyin was good?

But before he could get to his dait with Marg Snatcher, Terdo had to deel with yer pervinshul premeers, all of hoom had cum to Ottawar with their own shoppin' lists. Even Reamy Leveck was there, havin' jist bin re-alected by the same peeple that had give him a No-no flat on his referee-endum.

Terdo had bin hot to trot with a Charter Flite of Rites sints he first cum to the Common House back in his mid-sexties even though everybuddy elts was bored sick of him disgusting it. Them premeers was much more incline to Jokelark's "community of immunities" which took mosta the powers away frum the Federasts and giv it back to themselfs. In their minds Terdo was still the old tomcat among the pidgins.

The Snatcher

At the furst dinner up yer Redo Hall, hostied by the new EnDP Guv-Jen Ed Shire and his Lily, ther was rangling

✿ COOLINARY
FEETNOTE

Valeda sez it's
pernounced hore-doves,
and they're the little
itty bitty things you git
to chew on before the
reel fud is cumming.

even during yer horses ovaries.✲ Terdo's idees dint go down neer as well as the dinner. Even Newfyland's Briney Peckerford sed he'd druther hav Reamy Leveck's vergin of Canda than Pee-air's. Jeen Cretin pert neer threw up his peerogeys when he herd that. The only premeers that seem to be on Terdo's side was Ontaryario's Billy Davis and Nude Brunsick's Dicky Fatfeeled. The resta them premieres, yer gang of 8, seem determin to put Pee-air behind a ball with the saim number on it. Mind you, nex day, they all sign a cord that yer Bee End Ay Act could be patriotted as long as ther was a Mending Formuler attatched. (They noo it was broke and shud go in fer repair even if Terdo dint.) Leveck sined it too, and Clod Moron got him to give up his Cuebec V-toe.

Pee-air reely wanted to ride over them pervinshul suckers by takin' his case to Marg Snatcher eunicklatterly.✲ He had alreddy nocked up the Berdish Prime Mistresses #10 door the summer afore and presented his breefs to her. She didden take too kinely to his purrposal, on accounta them Berdish don't have no constitutional that's writ down, sept mebby that Maggoty Charter and yer First Freeform Bill. Terdo jist told her: "Hold yer nose and look the other way."

✿ LEAGLE
FEETNOTE

Ewnicklatterly, to be
downrite simple, jist
meens "Up you, Jack,
I've all the Rite I need."

Prime Mistress Marg tole him he hadda deel with her Privvy Counsillers if he didden like our BeeNay Act. Them Privvys tole him he hadda git agreement frum his premeers first. Terdo was desprit to git that old peece of paper frum yer Privy, and so he terned to Canda's Supreem Cork. Them Supreems in the red dresses tole Terdo that what he was tryna do was leagle but unconvenshunal, like him. They also sed Cuebeck never did have a V-toe to stand on. It only thought it had. That ment Reamy's hand was emty and he dint have a ace to deal away.

But the Supreems thought up a cumprymize. Pee-air didn't need to git anonnamuss approval frum them premeers, but he'd have to cum up with the John Handcocks frum morn two of them; say, mebby, sex. Terdo deesided mebby that gang of 8 wasn't all that impreggernabull, and he'd give wun more trying time to them Premeers. He hoped to git them to cum to their consensus.

They all met agin on Hellowean nite, witch is scary enuff fer a start. It was helled in the old Ottawar raleway station connected by a undyground tunnel to the Shadow Lorry, eh? It had high valtz of seelings with rotten acoostinks,* was now called the Nashnul Confidence Senter, altho' only Pee-air seemed to be the reel confidence man.* They was a snarly lot. Peter Lawheed was still sore frum Terdo's Nashnul Elegy polissy which tried to boil Elberta in oil. That singles act doomed Dome and terned Elberta's boom into a bust. I won't say Pee-air had never lift a finger to help them, but you ast ennybuddy frum Sammin Arm B.C. and they'll tell yiz it was only the middel finger.

The hole country could hear Petey's TarSands yell as he closed down yer Sink Rude. So Premeer Peeter was in no mood to waist time bumpin' his gums about Terdo's pet hobby, the constitooshun. Terdo felt the vicey of yer versey about the West's live-in standerds. Bein' a millyunair's son, Pee-air never had the leest intrust in Yewconomics, his own, or ennybuddy else's. That's why he speshulized in becumming a constitutional liar.

Nex day they was all on tellyvision. Nuthin' secrete

✧ ORAL
FEETNOTE

It's their own fault. We allways sweep our rottener coostinks outta the barn twice a day.

✧ UNDERGROUND
FEETNOTE

It was a Conference Center, not Confidence, and Terdo is not exackly noted fer being a Conference man.

about these meetins, everybuddy missbeehaved rite out in publick. Terdo purposed to Charter everybuddys rites. The pervinshuls still wanted a Mending Formuler in case of a goof. Pee-air called sitch a contrasept a "bone-us fer Seppa-rations." Everybuddy wanted a V-toe eggsept Billy Davis and Reamy Leveck who had alreddy bin fine-assed outta the wun he dint have enyways. Billy's Atturkey-Genrul Roy McMurky and Aln Blakey's aid-de-cramp Roy Romanose offerd a "not-with-standins" claws which allowed fer a rabbid "Hoppting-in" or "Hoppting out" of the clutch of the Ottawa hutch.

But that movement never cum to be passed. This kinda suggestiv maid the West nervuss. They didden wanna go to the poles over sumbuddy's elts's langridge. That nite while Reamy Leveck was sleepin' in his Shoddy-Air Hotel room over to Hull, them other premeers sat up late in yer Shadow Lorry eh?✶ Jeens Cretin still clames he wernt there, but the roomer goze that he was one of the fifth colyumists that rigged the new resolutions that nite. He's sposed to have Chopped Sooey with Roy Romanose in a kitchen on yer fifth flore with Ontaryo Atturkey Genrull Roy McMurkey (yer CF of L Tackle-that-was). Jeens yer Tuke, and Roy yer Uke, and Atturky Mickmurky is sposed to have cut a deel that cut out Cuebec. It cut out a lot more than that. Fr'instants: women, a minorty witch maid up mebby haffa the country, and abie-originals, always last on the Injun list.

Even that old P.I.E. farmer Anguish MacLain was haul outta his bunk.

There was no speshul statues fer Cuebeck, so Reamy pulled his pen away. He didden sine, he was fit to be tide; and Canda has bin untide insted of united ever sints.

✳ Shined, Seeled and Dee-Liverd

The Ottawar cerrymony ware our belubbered Queen sined the paper that pastry-ated our Rites was helled outside in the rane. Mebby jist as well, cuz Her Madge-isty mite have felt like Marg Snatcher when Pee-air told her to "Hold her Nose and Pass the Constitution." By this time, Iron Marg was too bizzy tryna git them Argenteeny grouchos outta her Focklin' Eyelands.

Shurely our Queen must have noticed our abridge-in-all peeples whoopin' it up in fronta her Bucking Ham's palliss fer weeks afore she cum over here. They was beetin' ther drums and whalin' like a buncha bandshees while her Coldcream gards was goin' thru the changes. The wun thing them naytifs wanted to keep was their connexion with the Birdish throan. But when they got back home Canda's First Famlys never got a look-in when putsch cum to shuv. "Nex time, nex time" everybuddy's bin tellin' them fer the passed few hundert yeers.

And what did that chartered liddle peece a paper do fer the resta us? Not vurry much unless yer a lawyer that wades thru all them whereasses and howsumevers and moreovers, and charges cly-ants an arm and a laig to do it. It sounds ta me like a make-wurk projeck fer them leegle-beegles. Undydogs who has a beef agin the guvmint are told yuh kin beef all youse want, but you'll have to do it in a Court instedda thru yer repryhensitiv in the Common-House. And if youse reely insist on gettin' stratusfaction, yuh may have to appeel yerself all the way up to them

Supreems. All Pee-air had reely dun fer us was to make free speech more expansiv*

Terdo should have quit bein' a Hed of State while he was still ahed. He went on to wirldly affairs like yer Norse-Souse questyun of whether plutocrap nations would help yer underware-develop thurd of yer wurld.* When he coulden git Ronny Ragin' or Marg Snatcher intrusted, Pee-air went on a peece missyun round the wirld, but the only thing reely hit the papers was when he ended up waring a barenoose in a Arb's tent dancin' sheek to Chic.

By now Reamy Leveck (or was it Clod Moron?) had desided that his Peek-youse party didden need Sovernty to keep up ther associashun with Cuebeckers. In fack, both Reamy and Terdo's kareers after this partickler pint seemed to be morer less yer Anty's climax. The two of them was Canda's Awed Cupple, almost as if they was eech other's alterd Eego, loose canons playing mostly on their full decks. They both agreed on the Big Questyun; they jist had differnt ansers.

✸ The Road to Mullruiny

Joke Lark was still around, altho' pritty much marked down on yer remainder shelf. Regressive Preservativs had allways bin good at back-stabbin', and when it didden work on them Grits, they went back to doin' it to their own. After Terdo was back in his offiss the Torys only had wun reel targit they wanted to consintrate on and that was their leeder. They got out the nives they'd used fer Deefenbeaker and Stanfeeled, and now they was sharpnin' them up fer their most recent preevious encumbrance. And the fella waitin' with the sharpest shiv was sumbuddy who had never held his seat anywares in that Common House – Joe's rivall frum the last horserace.

Mr. Moosejaw

After that lost Tory leedership convenshunal Brine Mulruiny's whinest hour had cum. He coulden git over that chinless Joker frum High River becumming the curnt Tory! Tory! Halleyloo-yah! Mebby Bullroney's expectorations run too high. Fer a neo-fite who had never held down enny bizness eggsept the Cam Puss Co-Wopshop at Sin Effects Universalty,* the kid frum Bake Homo had dun darn gud to cum third in a field of pert neer a duzzen. But that's not the way he looked at it: Briney Bullroney had expeckted to becum Primed Minster of Canda in wun swell foop.

But sitch was not yet to be. So getting into a Snit or a Huff (I cant keep track of them forn cars) he druv outta Ottawar leeving beehind his mammarys of pollyticks, and becum hed of yer Arn Ore Cumpny of Canda down to the cumpny town of Sheffervill. It was a blanched plant of yer Hanner "Mining Our Own Bizness" Corpulation of Cleeveland, O-hy-o. The job brought back mammaries of the time he was a little tad back in his cumpny hometown of Bake Homo, sitting on the nee of Chicagy Tribyune Kernel Mick Kormick, the cumpny town owner. Liddle Briney would sing the Kernel any song he wanted to hear ... fer FIFTY bucks. The Arn Ore job felt jist as gud to Briney as

❂ HIRE EDDICATION FEETNOTE

Sin Effects is short fer the colledge named after St. Fran's-Sis Ex-Aviater, a hy-flying munk.

sittin' on that old Kernel's nee, sept that this time he got a lot morn fifty dollars fer singin' the Yanky's toon.

While Briney was in charge, bay-smettles got hot on yer wirld markup and the price of them arn ore pellits shot through the ruff. So Prezzdent "Arn Man" Bullroney manedge to turn lossus into profets. Natcherly at the saim time them arn miners struck fer hire wages. Briney wasn't reely a biznessman, but he was still a nogoasheeyater in laber, and he brung about a settledmint that pleezed jist about everybuddy. Untill the price of arn fell way down agin, that is, and then that hy-priced laber packt didden look too gud to them malted nashnuls acrost the 49 parrlells of lassitude.

Brine musta seen the hand-rite-in on yer eggseckativ warshroom wall, cuz he quit the job jist as them Yanks wanted to pull outta Shefferville fer gud, spend their winnins at home and their fewcher investmints in ore pockits in Burzill. Brine couldna cared less about stayin' in the bizness. He didden want to be Prezdent, he wanted to be King. Wun reesin Brine was itchin to git back into pollyticks was that if Jokelark could becum Prime Minster of Canda, he figgerd ennybuddy could. But first he hadda close down the biggest orehouse in Cuebec and make everybuddy feel gud at the same time. He dun it. From now on call him Blarney Bullroney.

It was mebby his finest Briney-ist hour, speaking to them poor unemploid minors and tellin them about their genruss bye-bye wages.* He was sposed to have wined down his pitch after haffanower, but he went on tocking about the gloryuss fewcher in store fer Shefferville. He spun a tail about a noo big-inning with mangy-knees deepossits a liddle further north, and brilllium ox-hides a bit further

✿ SEVERANCE FEETNOTE

This was true: they could buy ther homes fer only a doller, which was about what they would be worth ennyway in a soon-to-be goastown.

north than that. Rite in the goastown itself, he sed, there could be a big Naytoes Senter fer training the Yerpeen farces, a ski-resort fer yer Intynashnul jet-setters, a nashnul park fer tooryists and their kids, and handy krafts fer the naytifs. The poor peeple lissening to all this would be lucky to have handy a Kraft dinner, but yood be sprised how menny of them wanted to bleeve Briney at the time.

No dout about it. The Bard of Bake Homo was reddy to go back on the stump and sing agin.

✳ Leederſhíp Preevenſhun

It was a yeer after Joe Clark got beet by Terdo that the Tory party put him on the grittle fer to see if he could still be their leeder. Ever sints Pee-air had got back into his swimminpool up yer SusSex Drive, there was a lotta wisperin' in yer Oppsit Position that mebby Joe wasn't the one to take them back to that prest-hideous address. And them missin' patter-on-edge appintments that Joe had never got round to handin' out before he was brung down by that no-accountant Crosby still stuck in yer Tory's craw. Patter-onedge was a bit of a sakerd truss to hardlime Torys and that's why they was bent on puttin' Joe thru the hoops, my deer.

They dun it at yer buy-anal genial meeting in Ottawar with 2 thousand Tory dallygaits chompin' at the bitch. The questyun was: "Do you think us Ingressiv Peeservativs should have a leedership convenshun?" After the Deefenbraker freeasco, young Torys like Clark and Bullroney had decide that there should be a kind of reeferendum on the party leeder every 2 yeers. So Joe was kinda hoist on his own pee-tard.

The upshat of the hole bizness was that sexty-sex purrsent of the vote sed they dint need wun, meenin' that Joe cud stay. Now when I went to skool that was consider secund-class honners. With them Torys I spose sexty was considerd making a bare pass.

Joe felt repreeved and releeved, and deesided to tuff it out with his cockus.* But them bludhounds who wanted him out was all fixin' to do it to him agin at the nex Tory convenshunal in Winpeg 2 yeers lader.

FEETNOTE

Yer cockus is pritty much like yer cacktuss, exsept with a cacktuss the pricks is on the outside.

Even tho' he was bein' a iron-bound capital-asst, Brine Bulrooney got hevvily involve in this on-cumming Windypeg Convenshun of yer Tory Follys and Spring Flaw Leedership Revue. Brine still clames he was on Joe's side, and he cum out to that friggid sitty in Janyerry fer to proove it. A lotta Medea peeple think he was at Joe's side jist to shuv in the shiv. That Tory Party Leedership Revue was plite on the surfiss but undyneeth it tern out to be a ring-tale snorter kind of a bludthirsty rang-dang-doo.

Dummest thing Joe dun was to offer to resine if he didden do better than he dun last time. When the vote was tabbylated Joe got the same answer with mebby a liddle tip extry, sexty sex point nine purrsent.*

✧ POPULARITY
FEETNOTE

Kin you imagine what a guvmint leeder would do today fer a figger like that?

Clarktorys cheered and figgerd they had wun. But Joe sed it wasn't gud enuff, and announce they'd have to have a open leedership convenshun pritty soon and he would be a candieddate. He felt he wanted to make sure he wasn't unwonted. Moe MackTier coulda kick her hazbin under his own seat fer quittin' with a cleer majorty, besides witch he had bin leedin' Terdo in the poles fer the last sexteen munths. But Joe was full of prinsipples, and kept troo to his wurd. Briney thought Joe was full of it all rite. He coulden bleeve his luck. Everybuddy waited around to see if Brine kissed Clark, becuz then Joe woulda had to give him thurty peeces of silver.

Nex Joon in Ottawar there was no short-edge of Tory hopes-fulls: John Crosbie had bin slavverin' fer the top job ever sints his blasted boojit had fallen short by 18 cents; Mikey Willson had bin in ruff Trade fer Joe but wonted to be in charge of everybuddy's Fiscal Affairs; Daisy Crumby, the Tiny Prefect of Tronto, jist wanted revench. He had cum to Ottawar as the most poplar little mare in Canada only to be froze out of Joe's cabnut. Peter Poxlington, former used-car and Hamway sailsman, now meet-packer and Edmunton Oily owner, cum with a flat incum tacks skeem that fell flat. There was Peeter Blakey, a mail-moddle Tory who would drop out afore it all started; and John Gamble, who was reely taking one, cuz he was far to the rite of Edie Ameen. And last to register was that also-ran frum a Tory leedership prevenshun ate yeers before, Briney Baloney.

This convenshun had the saim durty tricks with the round-in up of dally-gaits that'd bin dun before. All kinds of instanTorys and suppose-a-Torys was cremated on the spot. Crosby maid up foney Conservative campuss clubs and bussed them in frum yer Fur Eest as far as Sinjons. Jokelark had Seenery sittizens out to vote who had bin better off in ther beds, and Brine retalianated with twenny-five orfin children who couldna bin morn forteen. Both of them had Geeks jist offa the boat who couldn have tole yiz which candiedait was which. Briney top it all off by roundin' up all the drunks in Muntry-all tavs and swore them in as boney-fride Conserved-a-tivs.

By the time the candy-dates maid ther big speeches ther was only three seerious Con Tenders. Brine's was okay,

Joe's was better and Crosby was best of all. He got a stand-ing ovulation by promising to lern to speek the Garlic lan-gridge by 1995.

Nex day was the vote-in, and it look like Crosby was gonna git to be the first Prime Minster who spoke nun of Canda's offishul langridges. Ther was two farces workin' for him: yer ABCs (Anybuddy but Clark); and yer ABMs. But Joe got the first three ballietts, with Briney moovin' up all the time, and Crosby a distink thurd. Evenchly, Joe on the way down hadda face the same dilenema Brine faced the last time. He coulda bin Kingmaker 'tween Crosby and Bullroney, but he went the class root and let his peeple exercise their own french-fries. He never sulked neether, not wunce, fer yeers and yeers.

The Briner, dubble trubble

Briney Bullroney ended his campain for the Kingshit by brake-ing out yer Dum Perrynon. But he hisself had nuthin' but sody water. He wonted to stay cleer-hedded fer erly the nex morning when he would be nutworking his way tord his nex step: to git his arse on a seet in the Common House. After that, his agender was winnin' a Federast eleckshun and turnin' this hole country upside down ... or as he more likely figgered it ... rite side up.

✳ On The Jab Training

Pee-air Terdo was jist as anxshuss to git his Oppsit Num-mer lected to Parlmint as Brine Bullroney was fer to git there. Terdo thought a vergin Em-Pee who was sposed to be his cheef rive-all in the Common House would be a eggsellent targit. Elmer Muhkay pervided a vack-yume in Sentral Nova Kosher and Briney jumped in. He rented a log cabin mo-tell fer to make hisself look a bit like Abie-ham Linken, and pinted out to all on Sundry that he was a tem-puary Marmtider as he had bin at Sin Effects Universalty. So Brine tole the voters that as an old Antagonishticker it was grate to be home agin. I dunno how that went down in Bake Homo but all them Noo Glass Cows and Stellar Tons of peeple in Picktoe County thought it was jist dandy.

To putt a longstory into shorts, Bullroney had no trub-ble gittin' his Martime seet in Parlmint. His debutt there was a sucksess too. Pee-air give him a wellcum with a cup-ple sly cracks in between, and Briney reeply with a maid-in speech that was jist as good and even funnier. He give Terdo tits fer taps, and his tits tern out to be biggern Pee-air's tap.

But that was jist the hunnymoon. Nex day wholley acrimony began, when a Grit back-bencher asked Terdo a questyun about French-speaking rites in Mannytober. This was a delibrut set-up fer to git at Bullroney, on accounta the Torys in that province seem to be ded agin by-lingamalism.* Terdo noo

✿ RETRACTED FEETNOTE

Them rites had been give to the Mannytober Frenchys when they entered Conflergration but had bin took away a few yeers lader.

Briney was all fer by-lingamalism but probly coulden drag his cockass along behind him.

When the madder cum up in Questing Peeriod Pee-air maid a darn gud speach, but so did Briney on his ree-Tort. He had tole his cockass that mornin that ennybuddy disagreed with him would be sitting outside the Tory foaled as a inn deep-endent. Briney's stock rose over Pee-air's in the poles. But out in Mannytober them pervinshul Torys begun fillablustering agin bilingalism. Briney even got a cupple of unonnamouse deth threts, but he stuck to his gums and voted with the Grits. Evenchly he knew he would have to go out there and face them Mannytober biggits.

Bullroney procrapstinated fer weeks but finely went out to Winpeg acrost that red river frum Sin Bunnyface. He was greeted by sines saying "Go Home, Frogface!" but he stud his ground and tole them that he was not gonna go back on his party's histerical leeder. Briney remind them that their province had bin maid by-lingamal by the very Flounder of Conflagellation, Sir John eh?

With this stand, Brine dun hisself even better in the poles, so Terdo wocked into a blizzard cum Leepyear nite and cum out of it a ex-Prime Minster. Mebby it was the chill at them poles that Pee-air Terdo got wind of and not no blizzard outside the Common House that maid-up his mind in not trying fer a thurd cumming. He went up to Redo Hall, terned in his keys, then druv off in his Mercy Benz with a 24 yeer old blond in the jump seet beside him.

Now ya mind that Jonturner had bin in that Grit leedershit race back in '67 that went to Pee-air Terdo? If it had bin strickly a bewdy contest Jon woulda wun hams down, fer he was a blue-ide combynayshun of Pall Newman and Rubber Redfurd. But Pee-air was Mister Canda back then and runnerupp John becum Terdo's Minster in charge of our Infernal Revenoors. Turner up and quit sex yeers laider cuz he disagreed with Pee-air's pricey wage controlls. It sounded to me like Turner went frum Ottawar to work on a farm, cuz he sed he was going strait to yer MacMilkin' Bench. But it tern out to be a corpulent law ferm that worked outta a shiny gold building in Tronto, owned and oppy-rated by yer Roiled Bank.

Turner was in privates practiss, but wunce in a while he would send out a missal frum his downtown offiss and speer Terdo with the odd shaft. This maid him the Nummer One candied-date fer to succkseed his old boss in the eyes of yer disgruntle and even some of yer gruntled. By the time Pee-air cum out of that storm on Leapyers nite and called it quits fer quits, Turner was wading in the wings.

Pee-air figgered the fella that always looked like the driver of the getaway car in a bank robbry, Jeens Cretin, was a shoo-in to take over fer him. But when yer Jonturner step outta the polished woodwurk of his gold-plaited offiss in Tronto, he beet Cretin eezy fer

The clown prince of Grits

the job on the secund bullet of their leedership convenshunal. Cretin went back to Shawhinny-inagin and becum a best-selling offer with his book "Strait from Duh Harse."

With Jon Nape-yer Turner as our Prime Minster, the Grits were back on top of yer Gallopin' poles after 2 and a haff yeers on yer bottom. But the first thing Turner dun was to putt his futt rite in the doo-doo over that Manytober by-lingamalism questyun. He sed that sitch a madder was up to the provinces, not yer Federasts. Terdo must have choked on his dait when he herd about it.

Turner's second booboo was even bigger. He wanted to stand up that luvvly cupple, yer Queen and yer Pope, and call a eleckshun. His Holeness couldna cared less but the

Queen woulden budge. But Turner post-poarned Her
Majestic ennyways and snuck in his eleckshun shampain
ahead of her Roiled Toor. Then he maid nineteen more boo-
boos when he passed a list of patternedge anointments that
Terdo handed him on his way out the door.

Was Turner taking Canda to the poles to remind us of
the fack that it was rabbidly goin' to the dogs?

✸ Exercising Our French-Fries

The Tory husslers was hot to trot on yer husstings, and
they had a Big Bloo Masheen fer to take them ware they
wanted to go. Brine Bullroney wasn't carrying too much
luggridge: only 4 cleen shirts a day and a polissy paper that
sed "Hammer them Grits Good!" If he had enny fresh idears
he wernt takin' no risks in puttin' them to the voters. Wun
big risk he did take though. Insted of carrion on as the rep-
pryhensitiv of Nova, Nova-land, he wanted to be noan as a
Cuebecker, so he sed The Hell With Nova I'm Gonna Be
Koasher and git mysself nummnated in the ride-in of Man-
ick-u-waggon.

Now Manick-you-waggin inclooded his old hometown
of BakeHomo, but it also inclood Set Eels and Shefferville
and Lab Door Sitty, all of witch was now suffrin' frum the
shuttin' down of them Arn Ores Briney had bin in charge
of. 'Sides that, the ride-in was sollid Grit. But our lokel
heero wasn't deeturd; he could feel vickery in his bones.

Too bad he start off on the rong fut. It was all on
accounta Brine was sich a affabull sociabull fella. Pallyin'
around with the pressgang at the back of his campain-
plain, they was all jokin' bout the appintments that Terdo

had forced on poor old Turner. Mosta them was tired old Grits going to their reward in the Sennit, but the wun hand-me-job that had all them reporters dubbled up was anointing Bryce McKissassy as Embarse-adore to Porch Gull.

Briney joined in on the presslaffter, and wun of them ast him if he would ever give a job to a Libbral. Bullroney sed yes, if there wernt enny liv-in breeth-in Torys left without a job in the hole country. Then his face kinda crinkle up and his eyes twinkle up and out cum this jem: "I don't blame McKissassy wun bit. If it'd bin me, I'da stuck my nose in yer pubic troff with the resta them. Ther's no hoar like a old hoar." Now this was jist a joke and off yer reckerd, and them reporters all knew it, but sumbuddy frum the Ottawa Urinal, or mebby it was the Shittyzen, went and print it ennyway. Durty pollticks don't allways cum frum pollytishuns.

Them remarks blew a gasket in Briney's Blue Masheen, but then the Grits give themselfs equal time. Jonturner was follying the Libbral Party Precedent Iowna Pepyscola up the steps to a platform to make a speach when he suddinly give her a wack on her nether parts. It was the kinda bum-slap wouldna bother enny of Jon's locker room buddys, who woulda return it at the flick of a towel. But to a digglyfide woman in full frontal vue of a See-TV cammera, it set a lotta peeples on edge. Peeple nowadaze is touchy about this touch bizness. To give her credit Mizz Eyeowner give it to him rite back, pat fer pat. But the bumpatter-on-edge dammidge was alreddy dun, and wimmen started thinkin' about givin' Turner the back of their hand at the balliett box.

Briney appollo-jize fer actin' up like a old hoar, but Turner refuse to take back his bum rap. These are the thing that fokes remembers in histry, not yer reemers of speaches in Hansard. They remember Terdo saying fuddle yer duddle, or razing a finger, the wrong one, to us farmers when he ast why he should sell our weet. Or Joe Clark's goony laff durin' a debait when he coulden think of nuthin' to say.

Nex cum tock of a debait 'tween Broadsbent, Turner and Bullroney. "Honest" Ed yer End DP was as usual doin' grate in the Gallupin' poles, but not too hot in them eleckshun poles that reely count. Still, Big Ed was reckanized by yer genial pubic as the top dog in the House. But nobuddy had seen Brine in ackshun yet. Turner was havin' a lotta trubble cleering his throte and lickin' his lips, so he wanted to git the debait over as erly as possbull so the voters would have fergit all about his idiotsinkerseeze when they approached yer pollen booth.

Ed (Git the Hook!) Brodsbent

Ther were three debaits. Wun in French witch Bullrooney won hams down, on accounta Turner's Garlic was rusty and Broadsbent's was jist this side of Deefinbaker even tho' he was married to a Frenchfone. The wimmen's debait was won by Ed the Fed Socialite, but the other two male show-vizness prigs was countin' on the Anglish debait as the reel auckshun.

It was Turner furst brung up the issyuh of patteronedge, hoping to teeze Bullroney about bein' a old hoar puttin' his noze in the troff. But Briney had allreddy appalljized fer his gaff, and the hole subjeck suddenly backfire on yer John when Briney brung up all them 19 dissappointmints orderd by Terdo. Turner sed as a takeover Prime Minster he had no opshun. Briney pozzed fer the killerblow. "Yew had a opshun, sir. Yoo coulda sed no."✶

That debait was it. I don't care if a fat-lady sang er not, it was game over. Didden madder what happen the resta the time. Ther was hy-flyin promisses and gaffs and boo-booze on all three sides. And all the while, Brine's old pal Loosend Booshard was in the back room crematin' Bullroney's Cuebeck speeches that never menshun the fack that Brine was a Tory.

But that tellyvize debait put them Torys over the top cum eleckshun day with the thurd biggest majorty in histry. John Turner had bin around in a wirl fer 80 days as Canda's 17th Prime Minster, but fer now, Canda had cum to the age of Mullruiny.

✳ The Pollytícks of Ham Bítchín'

Yer Tory rayjeem begun well. The hunnymoon peeriod last-ed till after Valiumtime's Day when Bullroney had a luv-in with all the premeers out to yer Ragina. Even Reamy Lev-eck was all smiles (fer the secund and a haff that his smiles lasted). Them Westerers was delited with the new Accord when Energy Mistress Pat the Carny cancel the Nashnul Elegy Polissy. Brine also put a crink in yer Forn Devest-ments Revue Broad, and tole the Yanks that "Canda was open fer to git the bizness agin." He gave away all them goodys sted of usin' them as bargooning chits fer the Free Trade tocks he had in the back of his mind.

Brine Buloney set out his four pillers of Tory polissy: develuppment of yer Hi-tex, lower intrust rapes, on the job training, and free trade. He had never sed a wurd about this last subjeck on the campain trale.

This Ragina gather-in was mostly about yewconomicks but Briney hinted at anuther meeting comin' up that would convince Cuebec to join us on our constitooshunal and end all that bidder fewding 'tween the provinces.

There was a cuppla flys in the oink-mint after this "Luv-a-Tory" git together. Mikey Willson's notes fer the Tory secrete agender was left in a Winpeg hotel lobby, and ended up being publitched in that city's Free Presspaper. It hinted there was gonna be a big cut in everybuddy's eequally-ized tramsfer paymints. To add insult to perjury, a tape of a candlestine meetin' with Mannytober fine-nats minister Vic Shredder was maid by one of Willson's Aids, unoan to Willson and Shredder, and was only uncoverd when the tape beeped itself off at its end.*

It's only plite that yer tapee should be the first to know and be tole about it beforehand by yer tapir.

Meenwhile a new accord had sprung up in Ontaryo. The Torys was out after morn farty yeers but to do it, the Grit-hed Daisy Peeterson had to form a nervuss coley-ition with that silk-stocking socialite Bobray.

The new Federast Guvmint got its first skandle when the bran new Minister of Offense, Bobcoats, went over to Lar Germiny to keep Canajun troops on their NATOES. He end up off limmits having a tit-a-tit with a topless stripper. This maid him a secure risk fer sumthing under the covers. When Coats was forced to resine hisself, he was only wun down and lots more to go.

An abridge-in-all pow-wow in Ottawar terned out to be not so much wow as jist plain pow! when it tern into a shammels. Indidge-you-nuss leeders called Brine a raciest as they folded tense.

Brine had got as menny seets in the West as in Cuebeck so the nex big issue put him on the horns of an enema – he hadda big contrack that hadda go sumwheres. Canda had bought a Yanky jetsetter plain called yer See Eff 18, and its tail seckshun had terned out to be jist what it was cracked up to be, so it needed a lotta maintnunts. Our Offensive Department called fer tenderers to run a big bullion doller reepare deepoe. Biggest contenderers was Canadair of Muntry-all and them Bristle Airyspacers of Winpeg. Yer Winpeggers figgerd to be a shoo-in; they give the lowest bid and 75 sibbilant serpents in 3 federast departmints give 'em better marks fer their tecknickle progrum too. But when they open up the envelop, the winner was Canada Air. Brine's gift had stayed home in Cuebec and that Men-a-night, Jake N. Epp got the job of tellin' the bad noose to his fella Manytobans. Bristle started to live up to its name, and menny Manytobans are still snorting about it.✶

This reebuff started them Westerners thinkin' about re-forming yer Sennit so's they could git therselfs a bit a clout before they got clouted agin. They got such a complecks they started sayin' that even if yer Edmington Oilys beet the competishun all holler, under Mulruiny yer Stanley's Cup would still go to yer Muntry-all Canajuns.

The gratest try-ump fer Brine Bullroney that first term of offiss was yer Sham Rock Slummit with both them Rayguns, Ronny and his Nanny. Our Guverness-Genrull, Jeen Sovaig, was tole not to report to Cuebeck City becuz this was strickly a plitickle meetin', nuthin' to do with pomp under the circumstance. So she staid home in her re-dun Redo Hall and watched, like the rest of us, on the TV. Her

❀ CONTEMPTUARY FEETNOTE

The new nationally Offensive Minister, him with his overcoat throan over his shoulders like a opry singer, Marcel My-Ass, deecided to re-run this kinda sityation comedy. He wants to take the big Air Farce supply depoe in Downsview and move it to some outta the way place called Muntry-all.

jaw must have drop when she seen Ronny and Briney inspeckting the Vandooze Reggymen as Bullroney and his wife reely pumped up the pomp fer their roll moddles, the Rayguns.

Milla wasn't too ambulant, mind, fer she was expeckin' her nex liddle PC Junior. So most of the first day they jist sat around their rooms in the Shaddowed Fruntnack and dropped assid rain. Ther was free-trade tock too but not much of that got in the papers, fer the reel nitty-grit nogoshee-asians was to happen lader in the yeer with that Mortimer Slerd-lookin' Yank, Peeter Murfy and our own Simple Simon Reeseman.

Nex nite was yer Sham Rock consort, and it was glitter-in with Canajun talent like that fancy diva, Murine Forster, and them Fame-uss Peeple Plairs who do everything in the dark but make their oddiences faces lite up as they do it. Murine Forster sang a liddle Irish foke song she had lerned at her muther's nee, who probly lerned it frum those liddle nee-hy Irish foke, yer lepruss cons. That give Briney the cue fer to jump on stage and invite Runny Ragin' to join him in anuther old Hy-bur-neyin number. They was sposed to sing it together, but Runny hadn't bin reherse, and I dout if his mammary was good enuff fer the total recall of the leerics, much less the words.

The only fether in Brine's cap

So Briney sang the song strait into Ronny's face. I dint reelize it at the time, but he was givin' the Precedent of the Ewe Ass his assend on the Free Trades agreement, which had bin Ronny's idee in the first place. I still member the words that Brine was singin', tellin' us all about Free Trade: "AND THEY'LL STEE-HEEL YER ARSE AWAY!"

✳ Life's a Meech

Briney Bullroney felt offal good about his first meetin-up with them ten premeers on yer Meech Lake. Fer the only time in anybuddy's histry that they could all remember, there was yew-nonnamuss agreement amung all ten about lettin Cuebeck into that Constitooshunal, notwithstandin' the fack that Pee-air Terdo in his haist, had kep them out. Things was lookin' good fer Teem Canda Yewnited. But Briney had dun this by giving everybuddy a veetoe, and cuttin' down on his powers fer to giv to them provinces. Any pervinshul premeer is gonna be in faver of that. Sandy Claws hands out the candy and all the kids is happy.

This so-called win was alongside a lotta other losses. Mike-ill Wilson's first bludget tride to rejuice old peeple's penshuns buy cutting off their index and givin' them all the finger. Them gray powers didden take it lyin' down. They riz up outta their rest homes and they marched up and down in frunta the Common House hard by the Socred flame in front of the Toom of the Un-noan Lobbyist.* Brine got so annoid about this he made Mike Willson tern about face, take his pants down and put back on his sakerd truss.

Briney broke anuther eleckshun promiss which should of had him ridden outta town on a rale. VIA was conseeve by yer Grits ten yeer after Terdo becum Primed Minster.

Wernt long after that when the Grit minster Jeen-Luke
Peepin, hoose smiling face tride to keep us all in transports
of delite, cancel a lotta yer VIA rails, speshully way down
eest. Bullroney made a sollum promiss to his Martime con-
stitulents to bring back yer Atlantic Limited Service. But
when he got in the House his time-table musta changed. I
dunno what happen to yer partickler VIA's but ours got
shrunk by whatever in the aitch Preparation Briney uses.
Nowdaze them trains go past our place every wunce in a
while when they feels like it. Instedda settin' yer watch by
'em, you'd better bring along a callander. When it duz show
up, there's only one car fer passengers, the rest is all frate,
and don't expeck a conducketer fer to take yer ticket. Some
young fella moseys up frum the baggidge car and stamps
yer fourhed THIS SIDE UP.

A bigger stink was frum yer Toona. Pert neer a million
cans was passed by the Fishy Minster without so much as
the touch of a can opener until Army cooks started throw-
ing them fishys back. But the mane questyun in peeple's
minds was about Briney's role in all this. They ast the same
questyun that honted Trickydick Nickson at yer Watery
Gates: "What did he know, and WHEN did he know it?"
Briney happen to be innersent of all this, but his Pee Em
OZe offiss wasn't. They jist hadden bother to tell ther Boss.

But Bullroney got the blaim and his Fishy-
man, John Frazure, got the hook. Not so
much fer tainting things up with his deniles,
as fer counterdicktin his Boss.*

✿ BORN AGIN
FEETNOTE

Valeda sez to tell yuh
that sints gettin' the
sack Frazure now sits on
it in the chair of yer Key-
holes Peeker in the Com-
mon House. This is
where he gabbles and
plays with his mace.

A passel of other Cabnutters resined therselfs as well over other madders, including
Soozann Blah-Granola (expanse accounts in
tramsit); Andry Pissinet (flip-over land
deels); Mishell Grovel (jist plane skull-
drudgery); and Stinker Steevins (clames he

never tocked buzness with his wife at breck-
fust but left her a loan).*

After yer tooner stink-up, a cuppla West
banks went fishbelly-up and the deep dee-
posseters got reeimburse to the toonuva bul-
liun doller. Most taxpayers never notice sich
things cuz Banks don't stink like rotting fish.
This crisis was overseed by a woman, cabnut
minsteress Barby McGoogle. Everybuddy sed
she handel herself like a old pro.*

Then ther was that Maxy-prizzon in
Brine's own ride-ing of Manick-waggon. It
was sposed to have bin bilt at Drummerville
but Briney wanted it neer to his berthplace. I
spose that's so he could be close in his retard-
mint to all his old con frends who was ex-
cabnut minsters. This ment millyuns of extry
dollers in costs, and a lot tuffer fer the cons famlys fer to git
there to visit them up in Brine's boonys. He coulda sed no,
but he diddent.

But nun of them issyuhs becum parraymount when the
first Bullroney term got terminated. Ther was only one
questyun that Oppsit Position leeder John Turner wanted
delt with.

To free or not to free trade.

❂ BACKWARD FEETNOTE

This bunch seemed to reverse John F. Kenny's saying: "Ask not what you kin do fer yer coun-try. Ask what yer coun-try kin do fer you!"

❂ SHOWVINIST FEETNOTE

Valeda don't care fer that comparson. Barber McGoogle is allways first-class, as ennybud-dy who travels with her kin tell yuh.

✳ UP the Stump Agin

As the present encumbrance preepaired to go out on the rode fer his secund eleckshun, his proponents looked in pritty good shape. John Turner had gon thru the same ordeel as Joe Clark had ... a leedership revue ... but he had cum out the tuther side with first class honners, 76 purssent.

Ed Brodsbent was reely ridin' high as the most poplar figger in Canajun pollticks, and his party was rite up there first in the poles, standin' over yer Grits and well ahead of yer Tory. Ther was a lotta hintin' that after the nex all-partied debaits he could be the first Sociabullist Primeminster of Canda.

As much as the genial pubic was up on Ed the Fed, they was pritty much down on Lie-in' Bryin, and morer less neuterd about Jonturner. Joke Lark had bin kinda resussitated in his pullitickle kareer, cuz he had bin doin' a good job fer Canda looking into all the Forners Affares. Rejuiced frum Prime Minster to the top cabnut post, he joined yer Freakwent-Fly Club and never lost his luggridge hardly atall. To git back in agin tho', Joe was gonna have a tuff go in his Alberta constittulency of Yellahed. The fokes at home felt he had bin ignorin' them and spent too much time circumsizing the Gloab.

Runnin' agin him in Yell-ahed was a formidabull little feller called Prestone Manning. He was the flounder of yer Pree-Formed Party which had morer less replaced them Elberta separators of yer Westin Contraseptive Party.✳

✿ ALIENATED
FEETNOTE

Their slogon was "Pull
Out and Feel Safe."

Young Prestone was the son of Earnest Manning, who had took over yer Sociable Credit guvmint frum the lait Buy-bull Bill Abiehart. Dad Manning had run Alberta fer a quarter of a centurion till he went to his reward in the Ottawar Sennet.

Reeson his son called his new Party Pree-Formed is cuz the rools and reggle-ations was a ded ringer fer what was in his dad's old Sociable Credit cards. And young Prest hisself seemed a carbin copy of his Dad rite down to his looks and polltix. It looked like Dad Manning had got his Zeeroxes off. There didden seem to be no gin-ration gap in that family. It was "Father Knows Best" all the way, cuz his son beleeved in the importance of being Ernest. It remained to be

The beat goes on

seen however, whether Yellahedders would vote fer a man who looked fer all the wirld like CBC's Mister Dress-up.

There was all kinds of issyuhs to be disgusted between the candied-dates, like Meech Lake, yer deformed Sennit, yer growing defickate, yer up-and-cumming Valor Added Tacks which had bin so sucksessful in skinning the sheepish peeple in New Zeeland. But nun of this grabbed the voters by their balliett boxes. It was Free Traid maid this a one-issyuh campane. The big looked-fur event of the hole sex weeks had gotta be that big deebait 'tween John, Brine, and Ed.

Now ya mind Brine Bulloney had never been fur Free Trade. Five yeer erlier he had sed it would be the doom of this country. All it would do to Canda would be to close up all ther branched plants in tuff times, so's the Yankee home bases could score a home run and we would end up jist as the histerians sed we started, hoors of wood with our drawers in the water. Briney ackshully sed we lived nex door to a twitchy ellafunt and if it ever rolled over on us, goodbye Charlie. I bleeved him.

Some peeple now call Brine unprinsippled but I don't think that's fare. It jist ain't in his prinsipples to have enny prinsipples. He's a bit like that old Grit Mickenzy King who had no ideer what he wanted to do with Canda till he found out what Canajuns wanted. He wasn't reely the leeder of our camp, jist the follower.

It was Crosbie, Newfunland's anser to Archy Bunky, who brung up the subjeck of Freetrades during the eleckshun fore yeers before. That time Briney sat down pritty hard on him on it. But then they hired that big Grit Ronald Macdonald to let off a loud report on the state of our nation.* After milluyuns of dollars in expanses, Macdonald must have figgerd we deserve a treet today so he maid the suggestiv that we adapt Free Trade, recamending that we take the big leep even if we fell on our faith thru the Golden Arches of yer Ewe Ass.

Brine was now sold, without dout. Free Trade becum the panic-seeyuh that could save us all. "Jobs, jobs, jobs" is what he kept flingin' at us frum his stump.

Eds Broadsbent was now in the nashnul spotlite. He was the wun expeckted to rape Briney over the coles on this Freetrades issyuh. But it never happen. It was poor John "pane-in the-lumber-reegions" Turner who tuck on this assininemint. Unforchnitly John had bin havin' trubble with his cock-six all thru his toor.* But like a reel trooper he kep a stiff upper lip as well as his lower back.

Jonturner got his revench fer that other debait. He coulda pinned Brine on all his patteronedge appintments in

*CONSINENT FEETNOTE

I'm not sure if that wuz the clown's name. Valeda thinks it wuz Donald, not Ronald. He'd bin a sore winner fer the Grits in Rosedale, and then got Highly Commissioned by Terdo to go to Angland and live in Canda House hard by True-fallguy Square.

*TAIL-END FEETNOTE

In case yer wundrin', it's at the bottom of his tale-bone on the backside not the frunt.

the last fore yeers, and ast him why he never sed NO. But insted, Turner got Bullroney's back up agin the wall of Free Trade by imply-ing he was a traitruss Canajun and probly the aygint of a forn power. Brine sputterd like a old Jonson Seehorse out-bored moder. Ed yer Brodbent didden even git in his 2 senseworth.

Yewda thought that debait woulda clinch the eleckshun, but nosirree bob. It was advertizing wun the day, when every big malted-nashnul cumpny in Canda put big ads in all the papers trumping fer yer Free Trades. That turned the trick and dun in both yer Turner and yer Broadsbent. Brine was in with a rejuiced majorty, but a majorty nun the less.* Joe Clark was in too, but with twenny thousand votes lesson he got last time, and liddle Pressed-tun Manning was jist behind him, wella hed of yer Grits and yer DP's. A clod no biggern a man's hams was on the hore-izon.

☼ ACCOUNTABLE FEETNOTE

What Brine reely had was the most seets — his party dint get a majorty of the balliets cast.

Ed's D.P.'s cum in third like allways, and he was so shock this time he quit polltix fer gud and took up Yuman Rites. The DP's sprung fer a woman, Oddry Micklocked-in, to take his place. S'too bad in a way, cuz Ed was the only party leeder who was a granulated fillossifer with a post-decree in Yewconomics. His rive-alls had all got there by degrees* as corpu-lent or cortroom liars. Didden take John Turner long neether fer to give up his leeder-ship, and make waves fer Cretin to stop frettin and call in the Copps before Jaypoll Martin got started. But I'm gittin ahed on myself.

☼ POST NON-GRAD FEETNOTE

Not quite, in the case of Clark and Buloney.

The upshat of this eleckshun ment that Canda was in fer a free trading derangemint with 240 millyun Yanks, but nun with our fella Canajuns who lived in other provinces.

✳ Secund Time Around

First eleckshun promiss Bullroney took care of was anointing a Minster fer yer Environly Mentals. There had bin this big Axxon ile-spill up Alasker way hard by our North Waste Terror-Torys, and closer to Brine's home there had bin a big ruckus erly in the campane about a lotta PCBs ending up on the docks of his home-town. It was them PCBs that seam to be puttin' all them dyed-oxen in the water. Bullroney made a sollum promiss to git rid of all the PCBs in Canda within the nex five years. Then he went rite back on the campane trail and spent the next five yeers doin' his darndest to git all them PC sonsa B's elected!✶

Then ther was yer Glowball Warning about yer Greenhouses Defects. Didden seem to have no defect on our own greenhouse, but then I allways bank it with pig manoor in the winter fer to keep the wife's cold frame in heet. But it musta dun sumthin' to that big Greenhouse they Sprung fer out to Newfyland. It forced that Premeer Peckerford to resine hisself when he found out his cukecumber was starting to droop. The wife thinks the hole problem is cozzed by them Airs-hole spray cans goin' rite up yer O-Zone.

So Brine put all this yucky-logical Green Peas kinda stuff in what he called the cape-a-bull hands of Loosend Booshard. Nobuddy outside a Cuebeck noo who he was, but he had bin a old classy mate of Brine's at La Val, writ them

❖ OLYMPYAN
FEETNOTE

There'd also bin a Dumb-men ink-wiry in Tronto about them anal-bollocks Steereos which maid Ben Jonson piss away his Olimprick gold meddle.

speeches fer him, and was at that moemint livin' hard by yer Eyefull Tower as our Embarse-adoor to Fran's. But Briney brung him home, and set him up in a bile-rection in a safe seet up yer Lack Sinjon. If you thought Briney's campane promisses was extra-avvigant, you shoulda seen Loosend's. He maid yer Weel of Farchune look like a Down-at-heels Fud Bank. He had no trubble becumming a Federast Em Pee, and was into the Cabnut the nex day. Them as noo him wundered jist how Federast Loosey Booshard reely was, but Time would tell, and if they didden have the space fer it yuh could allways count on Micklain's maggotzeen or Sardy Nite.

Mikey Willson was still in charge of our fiscal affares but he had a bitta trubble with his bludget that yeer when he found he had sprung a leek even before he could put on his new shoes and present hisself in the Common House. A Glowball reporter, Dugs Small, give a prevue of

Mikey won't stand fer a leek

Mikey's bludget on his sexy clock noosecast, and was threttend with seveer rapercushions fer taking a leak on the TV. I dunno why they have a man in charge of our munny ennyway. You ask enny farmer who keeps the books and it's allways the wife and former sweetart. Besides wimmen don't gossip like men do. And a woman would never have a leek the way Mikey Willson dun; in the ferst place, she woulden stand fer it.

But this wernt what consern our Primed Minster atall. He was thinking about yewniting Canda over a cuppla weakends with the boys. A lotta things had happen since that yewnannimuss fun-gathering a cuppla yeer ago up yer Meech Lake. Fer wun thing, some of them ass-enting premeers was now outta their office. Noo Brunsick's Dicky Fatfeeled, Manytober's Howerd Polly, Briney Peckerfur of

Newfyland, and P.I.E.'s Anguish Mucklain had all bin replace by noo blud, Frank Mick Kenny, Gary Filament, Clide Welch, and Joe Gitz.

Don Getme was still quarterbackin' Elberta, and still insistin' on a TRIPLE "E" Sennit, but my gol, we've alreddy got a one: Elderly, Expensive, and Emfy-zeemick. In fack they had alreddy elected a Sentaur frum Elberta, Stan Waters, even tho' it wernt strickly leagel by Ottawar's rools. So he didden git to grab holt of his seat until mutch lader when Briney got desprit to pass his GST in the Upper-House.

Don Getme got sex hunnert thousand Elbertans out to vote fer a Sentaur, and the winner got 42 purrsent of them votes, which jist goes to show you that Stan Waters ran deep. Marmtide Premeer John Bewcannin' went to his reward in the Sennit soon after that and he sed that outside of the Nosy Kosher's ledge-islater, the Canajun Sennit was the nicest asylum he'd ever bin in.

✸ Yer Meech Breech

Yung Robber Booboorasser had bin the youngest Premiere in Cuebeck histry (twenny nine with the biggest ever majorty, 102 seets outta 110) untill he got Sepparated frum his offiss by Reamy Leveck. This was notwithstandin' the fack he had set up that big make-work projeck, yer Shames Bay. He cleered the land of Crees, and road hurd hard on the werk, which went through despike Axe of Sabbytadge.

Poor Boo had fled to Yerp after Reamy defeet him, and spent his time in Brussles studdying yer sprouting Common Mark-up. By the time he cum back home he figgered the best thing would be fer Canda and Cuebec to have the same derangemint. He run again, a decadent after his defeet. This time Boorasser beet them separators at the poles, eggsept that it was his Libber-all party that dun the beetin', not him. Bobby Boo-boo had blew his seet, and was force to stay in yer Expecterator's galley until a bylereckshun could cum along to sneek him back in the House. He got back in the back door in time to get to that secund gatherin' at Meech Lake. Trubble was he had riled all them other premeers by passing a moovement in his Dissembly that sed all sines outside stores in La Bill Provence hadda be strickly in yer Garlic. If yuh was a yewnicklingamal Yank toooryist, you'd have to go inside the shop

Robber holds his referendum

to see what in the samhill was on sail. Robert the Boo-boo musta thought this would be a sure fire way fer to git cuss-dummers by the malls.

Mebby this movemint got passed so rabidly becuz the most poplar tellyvision show in Cuebec that yeer was a buncha Brock Villains frum Ontaryio stomping on the Cue-bec flag. This dissgraceless incydint was give more re-runs than them Yank preechers Jimmy and Tammy Bakers ever had in their pammy daze. Terned out that mosta the flag stompers was ex-Anglow-Cuebeckers who had moved across the line into Ontaryio. But that kinda feeling spred a bit to places like Sue Sweet Marie and Thundermug Bay ware they went frum Buy-lingamal to only-English, after them two sitties got together and had a tit-a-tit (sorry! head to head) with each other.

When them 10 Premeers finely all got together about yer Meech Lake, it wernt up at the lake atall, but down at

Brine's place, 24 Safe-sex Drive. Brine got Milla to serve them all a supper, after which they drunk up till the weezemall hours of the morning and when they were woozy enuff, he figgerd he'd git them all to sine the peesa paper that would yewnite us all wunce and ferever. Us ornery Canajuns wasn't to git a look-in on all these mash-nations. Briney was treetin' our country as if it was a cumpny, and them premeers was his bored of directums. Us common sockholders was to be left out like the wife keeps her mushrooms, in the dark and cuvverd with bull-shit.

The two founding nations of this country didn't git so much as a procksy vote. I don't meen yer French and yer Anglish, I mean yer Mohawk and yer Cree. Seems like it'd be eezier fer Cuebec to git out of Canda than fer our First Famlys to git in on it. Meech was jist ten white men in blue soots bidding fer a little auction on the fate of our country and waiting, while loaded, fer the eleventh to roll his dice.

No dice. It didden cum off, yer Meech. Clide Welch was a constitushynal experk jist like Pee Air Terdo, and when it cum to sitch madders Clide and Pee-air was two pees in a pot. Clide sed he'd sine the blame thing but he'd have to put it to his house of dissembly as soon as he got back. Gary Filament sed he'd have to check with the other Many-tober leeders, DP Gary Door and Gritty-hed Shairn Carsteers, as well as the indiggin-us naytifs who had never bin kinsult about enny of this. The Constitooshun wasn't worth the paper them premeers sined it on if there was no unonnymuss agreemint. Thus endeth the last supper. Well, it shure was fer Rubber Bare-assa, he ain't bin back since.

And that drained the life outta yer Meech Lake. The Newfyland legible-laycher woulden even considder whether or not to pass it, but the deth-chop was give by the only Abridged-in-all member of yer Mannytober house,

Eelyjuh (I did it my way) Harpo. Wun shake of his eegle fether put the kybo on everything.

Well that dun it fer Loosend Booshard. He jined the noo kids on the Block Cuebeckwaz, a buncha fedralist separators who took a oaf to the Queen in the CommonHouse with one hand behind their back and their fingers crotched. It dun it fer Ontaryario's Daisy Peterson too. He had bin the hero of yer Meech-at-the-breach, even offring to throw in a sexpack of Ontario sentaurs to some of them have-nuts provinces out West. But when Peteyson declair a sudden summer eleckshun in the middle of everybuddy's vocation, his own province tern agin him and his loil serfs terf him out. Nobuddy was more sprise than that silky socialite Bobray, who suddenly reelize that he would be accountant fer all them eleckshun promises he'd bin makin' fer yeers and yeers.

Briney Bullroney may have bin flabby-gasted by all this Meech after-mass, but he didden have a snit-fit like ya'd expeck. He was too much in shock to do anything. Milla hadda take him up to Harrington Lake fer the resta the summer.

Wun thing fer sure, that no-no ment that yer Meech woulden inhairit the Erth.

✳ Yer Jokers at Oker

Wile our Prime Winer was sulking up the sun at the lake, the fertly-izer was about to hit the air conditionin' at a golf course hard by Muntry-all. The Oka town counsel wanted to expand their golf corse frum nine holes to ate-teen, and to do it they'd have to incroach on a sakerd naytiff burry-all ground. The lokel Gons-to-the Doggy Injuns put up a barcade to stop them. The Cuebeck pleece stormed it and in the frackass wun of their nummer bot it. We still don't know hoose bullit did it.

In turms of immeejit violins, this was much more seeriuss than yer Meech. This kafuffel had bin goin' on fer two senchrys, but the Ottawar guvmint figgerd it dint apply if it happend before the Fathers of Conflagellation wrote us all up. But it tern out to be the hottest summer we ever had. We was about to becum like Bayroot or Belly-fast. To think this all could have bin a void if only them golf clubbers had bin content to play the frunt nine twice.

The hole confruntayshin in Cuebeck started excalating. The Gons-to-the-Doggies was supported by their fella tribesmen frum yer Bay of Quinzy, yer Cocka-the-Wocky Injuns. They had alreddy had a cupple peeple die over Bingo and countryband cigareets a few munths erlier, but this had bin a sivvil war between Mohawk and Mohawk. Ther was a more millytant bunch amung them called yer Worriers, so-called cuz they was a worry to more reserve Mohawks. But when the call fer help cum up frum down the river, them Worrier Mohawks went on the wore-path and closed off wun of the britches tween yer Cubec south shore and yer Ile of Muntry-all used every day by thousinds of computers.

The problem sounded rachel, but it was reely more a madder of langridge. Them tribes spoke Anglish, not French, and some of their incesters had even help out that Wolf at the Baddle of the Planes of Abieham. Things got nasty. Sluburpinites frum Shadowgay, who had got tired of the britch-blocks bein' put to them, startin' burnin' a Mohawk in effy-Gee evry nite on the TV. English Canda started callin them Cuebeckers fashists when a buncha

Injuns in cars got stoned – not the usual way – but by these Cuebeck computers gittin' their rocks off in frusteration. They had bin inconveenced fer several weeks, but them Mohawks had had the same treetmint fer hunderds of yeers.

As he dun before with yer Wore Mezzurer's Axe, Boohoorasser called in a buncha Federasts to help him out: naimly the Canajun Army. But this shoulda bin Ottawar's consern frum the start. Cuebeck had no jury's diction over them Mohawks.

The summer before, Briney Bullroney had recall all of Parlymint to deel with a few Seeks and their camils who got unloaded hard by Yermouth, Nova Scoasher.* This time, Briney never made a moove. And neether did Jeens Cretin who had jist becum the Grithed in a convenshunal at a Calorie Stampeed out in Elberta. Both our nashnul leeders ducked outta site frum this mess, till peeple expeckted to see their pitchers on milk cartins as missing persons.

Valeda clames they was Tamils not camils, and they cum frum Sealon by way of Germny. They manedge to stay on in Canda too. Camils would never have gotten over that burrocrappic hump.

❄ Yer Bush War

It was only when George Bush went thru his Golf Crysis that Bullroney surfissed frum his summer sulk. I dunno what that crisis was about. Valeda thinks it was cuz he coulden git no caddy. I dunno a thing about golf, coulden tellyuh witch end of a caddy to grab aholt of. George drew a line in the sand when he got teed off, and his dog brung his balls back to him. We don't have the cable – the CBC still has our tubes tied – but I seen all this on the TV. George shouted to Millie "Heer boy, fetch!" and the nex day the hole Bullroney famly showed up at Kennedysbunksports. They wasn't invited, but I don't think George minded a bit.

Stars in Stripes

Him and Ronny Ragin jist luvs Canajuns. That's why they allways kept one in their backpockits.

I dunno what George and Briney tocked about after he spat George's golf-balls outta his mouth. They musta tocked about the sityation that was gonna put us between Eyerack and a hard place. Both of them probly agreed they could go to war agin Sadam Insane without consulting their own peeples. Then Briney offerd George three of our old destroyers. Bush thought Brine ment he was unloading 3 seenyer members of the Canajun Sennit, so he wernt too enthuse. So George ast Briney what else our navy had to offer. Brine jist sed "Frig It", and the subjeck was closed.

Nobuddy seems to noe witch wun of them brung up the madder of that Nooyork job as hed of yer Untidy Nations. I spose it's the old argymint about witch cum first, yer chicken or yer egg ahed. All I know is that George evenchly agreed it would be a good idee to let Brine do to the wirld what he'd bin doin' to Canda and what he should have bin doin' insted to his own wife.

I betcha George also brung up that Free Trades deel with Maxyco that he's so keen on, on accounta he wants to marry up our nashnul reesorses with cheep Maxycan laber fer to keep the good ole Ewe Ass on top in Yerp. Nun of his workers is neer so keen. I heerd yer Bushman copping a line of Bullroney's during his PrimeMary campane ... it

was "Jobs, jobs, jobs!" I didden reelize when Briney shouted that, he musta ment the other side of our border, and
mebby the tuther side of yer Reeo Grandy. And now he
expecks us to stan by while some Mexcan peon is paid the
saim rate fer a hole day as wun of our ottowerkers is
sposed to git by the hour. I'll bet you George Bush woulden
hezzitate to peon Canda.

Briney went back home frum Kennedys Bunksports,
but he shoulda gon strait to Hellfacts to wave off our sailers to the Poison Gulf, or at leest visited the secund frunt at
Oka. Insted he went to a Tory cock-ass meeting up yer
Gasp, eh? He sed there that naytiff deemands was "Bazaar"
in tryin' to set therselfs up as a indypendent nayshin. He's
singing a differnt toon now.

Mebby it was the thret of a hunderd Okas acrost this
country that deturd him frum saying more. Or mebby it
was the fack that our Supreem Cort had sed that Abrridge-
in-all clames before 1867 was still valley-id. And it sure put
a crimp in Cuebeck's clames of Sovernititty when they
hadda call in Ottawar's army to hold back the same clames
maid by a few Mohawk. Now ther Big Cheef, Ovaree
Murkaday is sittin at the constitooshunal table with them
Premeers, and naytiff wimmen is gittin' a place beside him.
Mebby we'll soon find out there's as many fractions among
yer Indigynuss bunch as there is amung us unsettled white
settlers.

The only thing Bullroney ever had to do with Oka was
when it was all over and they was rounding up 24 of them
Worriers into a bus. I think Briney planned to buss all them
rennygades to Ottawar and make them Sentaurs so he cud
pass his GST.

✳ Gouge and Scrooge Us

Mebby George and Briney had a little disgustin' groop about that GST tax Briney was all keen to impoze on us. I think meself it was all George's idee in the first place. He was pervented frum puttin' anuther tax on his fella Amerkens cuz he'd sed "Watch my hips!" as he shimmy'd frum side to side on tax issyuhs. A lotta Ontario-aryans now think that GST means "Gone Shopping in Tonawander," but it reely stands fer "George Sed To!"

Yer Gouge-and-Scrooge-Us tacks ain't my name fer it. First time I ever herd that prescription was frum the lips of a Tory private member who happen to be Chairman of yer Common House Fine Ants Committeed, Don Blinkern. He got hisself in trubble fer sayin' it, and mebby he only ment it as a joke, but he sure hit the nale on the thum. He also sed that this new tax would raze billyuns of dollars in extry revenoo, when the fella in charge of our fiscal affares, Mikey Willson, had sed it would be "revenyou noo-terd." That means it woulden raze enny more munny than the manufractured tax it had replace.

Well, it turns out the most unpoplar tax in Canda's histry has bin a runaway munny-maker, bringin' in tuns more of lewt than they figgered on, despike the fack that it has cozzed most Canajuns to runaway acrost the boarder fer to do their shoppin'. Briney never menshun this tax when he was askin' fer our votes the year before, he jist sed that Canajuns would be workin' fer change. And he was rite. After the next Free Trades agreemint gits sined up with Maxyco, and if he keeps on with this fool tax, we'll all be workin' fer small change, standin' on corners with our hands out askin' fer it.

Only bunch seems to luv this tax is yer chartabull accountants cuz they are makin' a good livin' on all the extry paper work this dam tax takes. And it's so inconsiste-nent. There's a tax on my milkin' machines, but nun on my hog feeders or my foul brooders. So you kin jist bet when that fella frum the Infernal Revenyou starts snoopin' round my place (to see how I'm doin' after I've been dun by him) I plan to be out in the barn milkin' my pigs and chick-ins. I think the guvmint's startin' to git the wind up about this tax, cuz last fall they took off the tax on sperm, witch has renude plans round our parts fer a nite depossitory. And Briney hisself deranged to git the tax took off single servings of yo-girt. I spose he wants sum Canajun culcher left on the table.

Wurst thing that blassted tax has dun is roon our nummer one hevvy industry. I'm not tocking about yer Ottopax, I'm deferring to tooryism. Summer before that tax was imposed on us, I maid a fare livin' offa the tooryists druv into the Taxyco gasstation next to our farm.* We'd sell them our orgazmic vegibles and the odd froots, and sumtimes even authentical Injun artyfax maid in Tiewan. Last sum-mer, nary a tooryist. I gess they didden want all that guvmint paperwork tryna git back that dam tax.

Canajuns was amaze at the anticks of yer Sennit putting their own block-aid to the Common House over yer Grab and Swindles Tax. Canda's biggist Day-Care Centre fer Seenry sittizens is the only Nashnul Mu-

One of the Ottawa Senators

seeum ware the fossils is still breething. But insted of the House of Doze, they was blowing their own horns, as well as kazooze, and other noisy-makers till it was NooYeer's Eaves every day in that Secund Chamber without a Sober Thought. But I dunno how them Ottawa Sentaurs is gonna be able to stand up in the NHL when they coulden even block yer GST.

✳ "We Shall Fite Them on the Meeches!"

Even tho he had lost his first constitooshunal baddle, Bull-roney was still determin to win the wore, not to menshun his next eleckshun. He started a new campane – yer Sunu-va Meech.

✵ INISHUL FEETNOTE

Valeda thinks that's the departmint set to reggle-ate a lotta culchured things in Canda. We used to take Templeton's CRTCs fer to keep ourselfs reggler.

✵ FREUDIAN FEETNOTE

They tole him too. "We want a job like you got! Sex hunnerd dollers a day pluss expanses!!!!"

This time devizing yer Constitooshunal wasn't gonna be a candlestine operation, but a democrappic appeel to all the peeple. He anointed the head of yer CRTC's*, Keef Spicy, to spend twenty eight millyun dollers crossing the country with his Ded Poet's Sassiety, asking Canajuns what they *reely* wanted.*

Cuebeck got busy commishunin' on ther own and they hadda coupla 'em: yer All-air and yer BlancMange-Compote. The first was compose of Cuebeck Librals while the ladder was a buncha Nun-Partisans. This meant that there was both Nashnulists and Federasts in it together. (But no abie-original, after all them ruckshuns at Oker.)

Then yer Feds cum back with yer Dopey-Bad-One commission. It had bin a Dopey-Castingate affare till the Clod
who give his name to it got sick of the hole thing.

Next was them cross-Canda Nashnul Unititty meetin's,
run by jist the peeple thereselfs. Awdly enuff, there was a
lot more harmoniums at ther meetin's than with the poly-
tishuns. First wun was in Hellfacks, and it was about
whether our country should have a weak sentral guvmint
with strong pervinshuls or the arsy of yer versy. The
ornery peeple's altitude tern out to be reel flecksible. They
sed if Cuebec wanted a lotta powers in their House of Dissembly, go ahed, but the rest of Canda wanted to keep
Ottawar in charge of most things. They called this Ass-met-
rical Fedry-alism. Reamy Leveck used to call it Soverntitty
Assosy-ation. Mebby they'll cumprymize and settle fer
haff-assemetrical fedderism.

The fewcher of Canda if yer Tory and yer Reeformed
Party and yer Seperators gits their way seems to be wrap
up in the fraze "Cums the Deevolution." That meens takin'
powers away frum Ottawar and givin' it to yer provin-
shuls. Frum watchin' Brine all these yeers it miten't be a
bad idee cuz my gol, if Briney Bullruiny had bin a agent of
yer C.I.O. or even yer Cagey Beejees he coulden have dun
more to roon this country. I don't think he dun it delivver-
atly, but if yiz don't know where yer goin' yer libel to end
up someplace elts. When Briney first got lected he sed:
"Give us twenny yeers and you won't reckanize this country." At the rate he's goin', it's not gonna take that long.

Terns out Brine was right about Free Trade and them
branched plants too. Now we got nuthin' but blanched
plants dyin' on the vine. To keep biznesses here, Brine's
Torys has took mosta the taxes offa biznesses and put
them on the backs of us individdles. Them biznesses is
leevin' ennyway and where is all our tax munny goin'?

Not to yer pervinshul guvmints that's fer sure; their tramsfer paymints has all bin tramsfured fer paymints sumwares elts.*

✿ DOWN THE
DRAIN
FEETNOTE

The munny's gone to pay off all them Nashnul Unititty commishuns. There cant be enybuddy left on salery in Ottawar.

An it's not goin' tord that defickit neether. Do you think mebby our bankers has bin advizing Briney what to do with the munny?! I don't think ther advice is worth a pincha coonshat after they give all them billyuns of lones to yer Rikemen bruthers without checking their co-laterals. They cant tock to us about rich wisemen ennymore. Peeple use to say, "If yer so darn smart, why ain't you rich?" Nowadaze they're sayin', "If yer so dern rich, why ain't you smart?"

The wun guvmint fella that seemed to have a deaf-knit plan fer our futures wuz that so-call fiscal experk, Jim Crow of yer Nasnulized Bank. Ya mind Jim Crow?* A lotta Canajuns mind him quite a bit. He's the one froze everybuddy's wages while givin' hisself a payraze of 35 purssent. He's the wun keeps puttin' up our intrust rapes so's he kin borry munny every Thursdy frum that buncha forners who are takin' over morn more of our country. And he thinks we should all feel good about it becuz as yer Crow flys, he's bin able to rejuice our inflammation to practickly nuthin' by doin' the same to our job opporchunitys. Sumbuddy should tell that smugsucker that Unemployment isn't Working.

✿ MISS NOAMERED
FEETNOTE

It's yer John, not yer Jim Crow.

Meenwhiles, them Yewniteed Nashuns has bin tellin' the wirld we're the absoloot best place to live there is. And everybuddy on this planit seems to beleeve this, eggsept us Canajuns. I git the distink impressyun that the ones with the most patterotic feelin's about our land is our newest immygrunts. They're the bunch singin' the loudest "O Canada's" these days. The Ministress frum Justiss, Kim

Camel, sez our nashnul antrum is too sexiest. She peefurs yer "Star Strangled Bammer." The wife sez her Parry Sound Sintenniel Quire has gone back to "God Save Our Maypole Leeves." That's becuz we live close to yer Gibson Reserves and we're gittin' nervuss round our parts about them abridgnall land claims. We feels self-unconshus when we sing "Oh Canada! Our home's on native land..."

✳ Epíc Log ... A Glowball Perspextív

Now I ask you, what's the good of bein' glowbally compet-ty-tive when we're on our way to becummin' jist the same as that Thurd of yer Wirld that's livin' blow yer slub-sis-tems levels? All them Yanks wants frum the resta the con-tinence is cheep laber (frum Maxyco) and cheep nacheral resources (frum us). All they seems to be intrusted in is what they calls yer "Bottoms Line." This meens we gotta put our bottoms on the line when it cums to gittin' down to big bizness. Them malted-nashnul corpulations don't stand fer ennybuddy's nashnul antrum – they'll go ennywares fer to make a buck and while they're doin' it, them devils will make us take their hindmost. They'll take their factrees enny wares in the wirld ware their bottom line is gonna cost less. Rite now it's Maxyco, ware yer Reeo Grandy is becumming a 2,000 mile Luv Canal and kids foreteenyeers old will work fer fifty-five cents a hour. But if the Maxycan peeons start to git orgy-nized and deemand more munny, them corpulations will jist pack up and go sumwares else. If Maxycan wages start risin' up, them factrees will jist move on to summers in Soused Amerka, or mebby Indie-Amnesia, Tie-Land, Bermer, Bangyerdesks, even Eestern

Yerp and (gawd helpuss) Maneland Chiner. What about settin' up in yer farmer Serviet Onion, witch is tryin' like
desprit to be free enterprizin' capitolists? Or slub-topical
Affricker with is alreddy starvin' without enny starvation
wages?

They're crematin' all this mess in the name of "Glowball Compy-titian" but what them Bottomliners is reely
lookin' fer is anywares away frum pryin' eekylogical eyes
and guvmint taxmen. Sitch things is consider to be obstick-
les to prospairity.

Funny thing in all this is while all them Roosian Reds is
tryna git to be free-swingin' Kapital-ists, our bunch is goin'
backwerds and tryna set up what looks like that old Middle
Aged Fewtile Sistern! There's yer big biznessmen acting
like forteen-senchry dooks and barns, raiding eech uther's
feefs or morn likely ganging up in keyhoots with eech uther
to hire the cheepest surfs. Big biznesses are now homeless,
bounderyless, and roamin' the gloab lookin' fer that Bot-
tomline like it was yer Holy Grale.

So what kin us liddle guys do agin these rubber barns
operatin' outside our leegle limits? We can't be the wirld's
pleeceman ... even the States has give up on that. But
mebby we kin still pleece what goes on inside our own
boarders. Them extry-trestial cumpnys may do their dirty
work outside our 200-mile zone, but most of them still
holes up here in ther homes cuz it's still the nicest place in
the world fer to live. They're loil Canajuns when it soots
them, but if their profets cums frum exploiting forn child
laberers or pollyuting sumbuddy eltses environly-mentals
in the naim of free trades, we should be able to get at 'em
fer it. What we need is a Glowball minnymums wage law.
We gotta git togither to push the world's bottoms up, not
pull their tops down.

And what about posterity, witch is jist around the cor-

ner? Where is all this lazy-fairy, lowest cum-on deenomi-
nater stuff gonna end? In sum robottick fackery in
Antarticker soopervise by one King Pengwin??? Then what
happins? Do we start this hole re-cycle all over agin? What
goes down cums round, as they say. Histry has a way of
repeeting on itself. It's too bad nobuddy pays any mind to
us histerians. Becuz we have seen the past, and it works.

✸ Ware Credit is Doo